SPICE AT HOME

In the memory of Roger Looker, for his friendship, wisdom and support. Roger, your 'Spirit in Life' will forever be an inspiration and example for us.

SPICE
AT HOME

VIVEK SINGH

First published in Great Britain in 2014 by
Absolute Press, an imprint of Bloomsbury Publishing Plc

Absolute Press
Scarborough House
29 James Street West
Bath BA1 2BT
Phone 44 (0) 1225 316013
Fax 44 (0) 1225 445836
E-mail office@absolutepress.co.uk
Website www.absolutepress.co.uk

First reprinted 2014

Publisher Jon Croft
Commissioning Editor Meg Avent
Project Editor Alice Gibbs
Art Director and Designer Matt Inwood
Assistant Designer Kim Musgrove
Editor Gillian Haslam
Photographer Lara Holmes
Recipe Tester Genevieve Taylor
Props Stylist Jo Harris
Indexer Ruth Ellis

A catalogue record of this book is available from the
British Library

ISBN: 9781472910905

Printed and bound in Spain by Tallers Gràfics Soler

A note about the text
This book is set in Minion and the headline fonts are in
Orial. Minion was created by Robert Slimbach, inspired
by fonts of the late Renaissance. Orial is a striking
contemporary font designed by Salman Boosty.

Bloomsbury Publishing Plc
50 Bedford Square, London WC1B 3DP
www.bloomsbury.com

Bloomsbury is a trademark of Bloomsbury Publishing Plc

CONTENTS

MY HOME COOKING

Home is where everyone first experiences food. It shapes their memories, likes and dislikes. Most people's understanding of family and community is shaped through their experiences of food, of celebrations big and small, so much so that food even shapes people's personalities to some extent. Most people's introduction to food and the joy it brings, begins at home but one thing I have begun to appreciate more and more recently is how 'home cooking' is rapidly changing with the changes in lifestyle, with travel and migration, and the changing socio-economic climate each day.

For example, my home cooking is very different from my mother's. I still remember the time in 1970s in a colliery near Asansol, West Bengal, when she used to cook on a coal fire, 3 or 4 full meals for the 5 of us each day, prepared from scratch using only the freshest ingredients bought from the vegetable market or the sellers that would bring produce to sell at our door-step.

We didn't have a refrigerator, so shopping had to happen every day, sometimes twice a day. There was nowhere to store left-over food, so we were encouraged to finish everything on our plates and wasting food wasn't an option.

Guests, relatives, friends and other visitors would often arrive unannounced and stay on for weeks, frequently more guests would join in for the odd meal and my mother would conjure up dishes to feed everyone, as though by magic! I have a huge amount of respect for her flexibility, innovation and ingenuity in being able to come up with enough food to feed so many at such short notice.

Fast forward to today, cooking has changed significantly. Ingredients are easier to source, better prepared and packed, and storing leftovers has also become easier. It has become easier to plan and prepare as folks tend not to drop in unannounced so much either!

Joking aside, I look at the kind of cooking that goes on in our household in London and it couldn't have been more different. For one, it may appear crazy but the amount of international influence in our home kitchen today would be unimaginable a few years ago. Partly through travel, and partly because of the melting pot of different cultures that is London, we have access to the whole world's ingredients in Britain. I must admit, my being a chef must also have some bearing, but really, most of the cooking at home is still done by Archana! I am myself surprised sometimes how seamlessly the menu at home changes from Italian (Keralan Spiced Seafood Linguini) to Thai (Tom Kha Gai), to a French-inspired Pithivier, to Chinese (Toffee Banana) and then closer to home to those eternally familiar parathas with a variety of fillings.

Some things don't change however. Whether it's a regular meal at home, or a sibling's birthday when 20 of their friends have arrived for evening snacks, the birth of a relative's child, or celebrating Holi or Diwali or one of the other hundreds of festivals with friends and neighbours, food was, and is, at the centre of all these celebrations and is in many ways the unifying factor.

When I think back to my mother's cooking when I was a child, I don't know how much of it was a pleasure and how much of it a challenge for her. But I know for sure that in the world that we live in, where people work hard and have little time for themselves, the act of cooking for others, of entertaining, is an act of ultimate generosity and needs to be a pleasure for everyone involved.

It's important for some people to put on a great show, a big spread and the most elaborate, thought-through event. I know people who plan things meticulously, following recipes and timings to the letter. Such precision helps, but it's not more important than pleasure.

I place much more importance on pleasure when cooking at home, so don't get too worked up about perfection or precision and get stuck in.

PRACTICE

I remember reading a quote from Bruce Lee somewhere and he said: 'I fear not the fighter who has practiced a hundred moves once, but the fighter who has practiced one move a hundred times'.

Pick a few dishes that you like the sound or look of and try cooking them several times until you feel you've really got the hang of it, and the recipe has become a friend.

I also remember being on BBC's *Saturday Kitchen* with James Martin and John Torode. I was cooking chargrilled partridge with peanut and dried mango. James saw me spicing the marinade and commented on how easy I made it look. Whenever James tried to recreate a recipe of mine, his results weren't quite the same. At that point John Torode said something I will always remember. He said that just because we learn to read music doesn't guarantee we could play a piece from Mozart or Beethoven and it would sound the same! It requires practice, and one should be prepared to give that time, at least to those recipes we like the sound of and wish to make our own.

I suggest trying the same dish a few times before moving onto the next. Practice does make perfect and it goes a long way in building confidence as a cook. You could also try cooking the same ingredient in a few different ways. That way, you give yourself a chance to really get to know the ingredient well and make it a friend.

Another thing that really helps while cooking things first time around are the techniques of touch and taste. When grinding spices, roasting, crushing, cooking, seasoning, use your fingers where possible, use touch as a guide, and taste, taste, taste all along. With the exception of raw chicken, most other spices, vegetables, meat and seafood can be tasted throughout the cooking process. Regular and frequent tasting of the cooking vegetables, smelling of the roasted spices, tasting of the marinated meats etc. allows your brain to map the transformation of ingredients and helps you when you're cooking the dish next time round.

BASICS

Do invest in a good knife and a decent chopping board, they will go a long way in enhancing the experience of cooking. Depending upon how much you cook, a good peeler, a small paring knife, perhaps a temperature probe, a timer, a good weighing scale, and decent colander/ strainer could all come in very handy too. It's not about spending lots of money, more about planning ahead, as having them to hand makes cooking at home a lot easier and more fun. As always the devil lies in the preparation!

When you first start off with this book, you may find a lot of the recipes more suitable as weekend recipes. I hope that as you become more familiar with them, they become friendlier and you could put them together on a busy weekday too.

For me, home cooking is also about utilising every last bit of produce or ingredient that you've spent good money on. I particularly like reusing leftovers, extending them with the addition of other ingredients, and turning them into new dishes that are meals in their own right, for example leftover Rogan Josh of Lamb Shanks (pages 112–113) gets turned into a Pithivier (page 114), a French-inspired puff-pastry pie, or the leftover Butter Chicken (page 102) gets a new avatar as a Ravioli (pages 154–155). So much so, I like having some grilled chicken tikka in the fridge all the time, so I can rustle up a quick grilled chicken and chilli sandwich any time of the day or night.

I also like the flexibility of having simple ingredients prepped and lying in the fridge, like a simple ginger and garlic paste, made by blending equal quantities of peeled ginger and garlic cloves in a blender.

SPICES

Spices are the thing that most defines Indian cooking, whether in homes or in hotels. There isn't another cuisine or culture in the world that uses spices in so many ways, and so many myriad combinations as Indian food. India is the largest producer and consumer of spices, and has a tradition of using spices that goes back thousands of years. Linked to the knowledge of 'Ayurveda': 'Ayur' meaning 'Life', and 'Veda' meaning 'the knowledge of'.

This knowledge of life in ancient Indian scriptures teaches us the use of spices for various uses: for flavour, colour, taste, texture, preservation (i.e. prolonging the shelf life of ingredients) and for medicinal and religious purposes.

We use cumin seeds to aid digestion; coriander seeds and leaves to bring down body temperature; fennel seeds as a digestive and a mouth freshener; ajowan or carom seeds to soothe the stomach and to cure colic in young children. Fenugreek seeds are considered to be a very potent blood purifier and are believed to bring down blood cholesterol as well as being an effective antidote for those suffering from diabetes. Turmeric is an effective antiseptic and builds up the body's defence against wounds and aids healing. In fact turmeric is considered auspicious in most Hindu households. The only time Hindus exclude turmeric from their cooking is when the family is in mourning.

But on the whole, spices in Indian food, as per 'Ayurveda', are not considered cures as much as they are considered as a prevention for certain ailments.

As beneficial as they can be, spices are also probably the most intimidating aspect of Indian cooking. People often are put off by ingredient lists the length of their arm, the tedious preparations involved and the complexity of the dish itself. It really doesn't need to be like this.

AS EASY AS 1-2-3

Introducing spices into your everyday cooking should be as easy as 1-2-3 really.

I like to think of spices in clusters of 1, 2 and 3. Cluster 1 would include cumin seeds, coriander seeds, fennel seeds, ground red chilli powder, ground turmeric and black peppercorns. These six spices along with salt are a good way to get introduced to spices and you can make hundreds of varieties of dishes before you need more friends.

The second cluster of spices could include slightly more expensive, but also special, spices like green cardamom, black cardamom, cloves, mace, nutmeg, cinnamon and star anise. These spices are more aromatic, all go into making a good garam masala, they keep well and travel well and were an integral part of the spice trade for centuries.

The third cluster could include expensive spices such as saffron, uncommon aromatics such as screw pine essense, rose water and rose petals, and less popular spices such as fenugreek seeds and leaves, carom seeds and nigella seeds (a brilliant match with fish and seafood) or even the lesser known black stone flower or rock moss. At this point you've long crossed the territory of spice enthusiast and are bordering on becoming a spice geek!

Black stone flower, or lichen, can usually be found to buy online, and although it does not have a prominent taste or flavour of its own, it's a very effective flavour fixer, like a conductor in an orchestra, bringing out a symphony of spices which is greater than the sum of its parts.

BUYING AND STORING SPICES

As a general rule, it's best to buy your spices whole and store them in an airtight container, away from light, in a cool, dry cupboard.

The exceptions to this rule are ground red chilli powder and ground turmeric. These two spices can and should be bought ground, as it can be messy making your own and the quality does not vary much.

Depending upon how much cooking you do, you may buy ground cumin and coriander seeds, but if you don't use much, I recommend grinding small quantities of your own.

All other spices are best bought whole and ground as needed. Depending upon the use, you may choose to simply dry the spices by placing them on top of an oven overnight or placing for 30 seconds to a minute in a microwave. Alternatively, in some cases, like a Kadhai spice crust, you may lightly roast the spices in a dry frying pan to bring out a roasted nutty flavour from the spices. Once ground, you can store any leftover spice mixes in an airtight container away from light for 3–4 weeks at most after which the spices lose most of their perfume/aromas.

As far as using spices is concerned, there are a few things worth bearing in mind. Normally, whole spices are added to hot oil or ghee at the beginning of cooking a dish, allowing the spices to crackle, pop and release their essential oils and flavours in the cooking medium which then ensures the flavours are distributed evenly throughout the dish. Relatively cheap ground spices such as cumin, coriander seed, chilli powder and turmeric are used during cooking; they add flavour, colour, body to the dish.

Aromatic spices such as mace, nutmeg, cardamom and garam masala are used at the very end, like a seasoning, a finishing spice. So if you get the drift, the more expensive the spice, the more sparingly it's used and added last for best appreciation of its flavours.

One of the downsides of the British familiarity with certain Indian dishes is that things are turned into a formula. For example, here in Britain, we refer to a Kadhai, a Madras, a Dhansak, a Rogan Josh, so on and so forth. When I first arrived in the UK in 2001, I was bemused and slightly lost as to what that really meant. Here, I have tried to give out the different spice combinations that make these dishes unique (refer to Spice Maths, pages 10–11).

Finally, as much as this book is about the kind of dishes I grew up with, and the kind of dishes we now cook in our London home, it's also about introducing spice into the kind of dishes you're familiar with and cook in your home.

For example, poories and tomato chutney was a childhood favourite of mine when I was growing up and Jhal Muri – a simple street snack sold by street vendors in Asansol – now features with cured salmon, an addition from my years of living in England.

My mother-in-law makes the very best poha – a simple Indian breakfast using pressed rice flakes cooked with potatoes and peas. It could make a welcome addition to your breakfast repertoire.

Even though I mostly had the grilled chicken and chilli sandwich as a very late-night snack when I was a student in Delhi, I often reminisce about the old days by making it for a quick and easy lunch. My team in Cinnamon Soho always make it for my lunch if I'm there and have put it on their lunch menu.

You will also find long-standing favourites like roast chicken, chicken wings and spice-grilled sardines, all sitting comfortably alongside my mother's signature malpuas – deep-fried pancakes that are great both for breakfast or as a dessert.

Cooking at home is changing, as is everything else in our lives, and it's about to change again.

Vivek Singh, London
June 2014

SPICE MATHS

Spice mixes aren't complicated codes.
Here are easy sums to create the foundations
for a variety of dishes.

KADHAI SPICE MIX
Cumin seeds + coriander seeds + dried red
chillies + fennel seeds + black peppercorns

KORMA SPICE MIX
Cloves + bay leaf + cardamom
+ mace + cashew nuts

VINDALOO SPICE MIX
Cumin seeds + black peppercorns + dried red
chillies + cloves + cinnamon

ROGAN JOSH SPICE MIX
Cinnamon stick + black cardamom + cloves +
bay leaf + asafoetida + ground ginger + dried
red chillies + black peppercorns + rattan jyoth

DHANSAK SPICE MIX
Dried red chillies+ black peppercorns +
nutmeg + cloves + fenugreek seeds + asafoetid

ACHAR PICKLE
Cumin seeds + fenugreek seeds + mustard
seeds + onion seeds + fennel seeds

Kadhai Spice Mix

Rogan Josh Spice Mix

Korma Spice Mix

Vindaloo Spice Mix

Dhansak Spice Mix

Achar Pickle

TO START
THE DAY

POORIES

Poories, or *luchis* as they are called in Bengal, are the same thing, except that in Bengal they use a tad more oil or ghee when making the dough which makes the breads shorter and crisper. They also use refined flour rather than wholewheat flour, as is the norm in the rest of the country. Finally, Bengalis like to use onion seeds and ajowan in their bread which makes it dramatic in appearance, more flavoursome to eat, and easier to digest! Feel free to use only wholewheat flour if you wish – it's much better healthwise.

MAKES 20

500g plain flour or chapatti flour
(or half and half)
2 teaspoons salt
1 teaspoon sugar
1 teaspoon ajowan seeds
1 teaspoon nigella seeds
1 tablespoon ghee or vegetable oil
2 tablespoons vegetable oil, for rolling,
plus extra for frying

Mix together the flour, salt, sugar and seeds and then rub in the ghee or oil with your fingers, to incorporate well into the flour. Make a well in the centre of the flour and make a stiff dough by pouring in 225ml cold water little by little. Work the dough well with your hands, then cover with a damp cloth and set aside for 15 minutes.

Divide the dough into 20 pieces and rest it under a cover for another 5 minutes.

Heat a deep fat fryer to maximum heat or simply heat the oil in a wok.

Taking one piece of the dough at a time, shape it into a smooth ball. Apply a little oil on the dough and roll out on a smooth surface using a rolling pin to make a circular disc approximately 10cm in diameter.

Deep fry the poories in hot oil for 4–5 minutes until crisp and golden and they puff up.

This is an excellent accompaniment to dry curries and is very popular with children as a snack or a picnic bread. My favourite accompaniment to *luchis* is a sweet tomato chutney or hot sweet pumpkin pickle.

POHA

This is the greatest spiced breakfast ever – well, certainly in our household as no one makes this quite like my mother-in-law, Geeta, does. I don't eat poha made by anyone else!

SERVES 4

200g pressed rice flakes (called *powa* in Asian grocers)
4 tablespoons vegetable or corn oil
20 curry leaves
1 tablespoon mustard seeds
2 red onions, finely chopped
2 medium potatoes, peeled and cut into 1cm cubes
1½ teaspoons salt
1 teaspoon ground turmeric
1 teaspoon sugar
4–5 green chillies, finely chopped
75g frozen green peas (optional)
50g coriander leaves and stalks, chopped
juice of 1 lemon
100g roasted peanuts or Bombay mix, to garnish

Soak the rice flakes in hot water for 1 minute, then drain and rest in a colander for 10 minutes.

Heat the oil in a wide casserole or wok, add curry leaves and mustard seeds and let them crackle and pop. After a minute or so, when the sizzling subsides, add the onions and sauté for 2–3 minutes, then add the diced potatoes, salt, turmeric, sugar and green chillies and cook for 6–8 minutes over a high heat until the potatoes are cooked and the onions begin to caramelise slightly at the edges. Stir to mix properly, cover with a lid and reduce the heat for a couple of minutes if the potatoes need more time.

Once the potatoes and onions are cooked, add the green peas, if using them.

Next add the soaked rice flakes. Mix carefully to avoid breaking the flakes. Cook for 2–3 minutes until heated through. Sprinkle with coriander and finish with a squeeze of lemon.

Divide between four plates and serve sprinkled with roasted peanuts or Bombay mix. The spicy but crisp garnish adds texture.

SMOKED HADDOCK KICHRI

The classic Anglo-Indian dish of kedgeree derives from the popular *kichri* – rice and lentils cooked together with ginger, chillies and onions. The British in India during the days of the Raj adapted the dish by adding eggs (which were easily available) and smoked fish (which had a longer shelf life), and the recipe made its way home with them as this breakfast dish. Traditionally the eggs are just boiled and flaked into the rice, and the lentils have been lost with time. If you wish, the rice can be cooked the day before and kept in the fridge overnight.

SERVES 3-4

200g undyed smoked haddock
milk, for poaching
2 tablespoons vegetable oil
1 white onion, finely chopped
2.5cm piece of ginger, finely chopped
2 green chillies, finely chopped
1 tomato, deseeded and chopped into 5mm dice
1 teaspoon ground turmeric
75ml fish stock or hot water
500g boiled basmati rice (uncooked weight 170g)
1 teaspoon smoked sea salt (regular salt will do too)
4 hard-boiled eggs, the whites chopped, and yolk discarded
1 tablespoon chopped coriander
30g butter
2 tablespoons single cream (or 2 tablespoons of the poaching liquid)
freshly ground black pepper

To poach the fish, place in a frying pan with enough milk to cover it to a depth of 1cm. Add a small knob of butter and a grinding of black pepper, cover tightly with foil and poach for 3–5 minutes, depending on the thickness of the fish. Remove the fish from the poaching liquid, allow to cool, then flake into large pieces. (If you wish, this can be done the day before.)

Heat the oil in a large frying pan, add the onions and sauté for 15 minutes over a low-medium heat until golden brown. Add the ginger, chillies and tomato to the pan and stir to mix well. Add the turmeric and continue to cook for a minute, then add the fish stock or hot water. Toss in the boiled rice, then add salt to taste. Fold in the chopped egg whites and flaked haddock and sprinkle in the coriander leaves. Gently stir in the butter and cream and remove from the heat.

Serve into bowls, grind a twist or two of black pepper over the top and eat immediately.

BOMBAY SCRAMBLED EGGS

Bombay scrambled egg is the most popular breakfast dish we serve at The Cinnamon Club. This spicy scrambled egg is very popular on the Indian sub-continent and is an all-day treat, usually eaten with bread or parathas (layered bread). At The Cinnamon Club we serve it with tawa parathas, but it tastes just as good inside a soft white bun or even a brioche.

A fine example of traditional street food in Bombay, this is what fuels most of the city in the morning. The spice kick, combined with scrambled eggs and fresh herb flavours, is a good way to wake up your system and start the day. We're pleasantly surprised to see a Mumbai working man's breakfast go down so well in Westminster!

SERVES 4

10 eggs, beaten
4 tablespoons vegetable oil or salted
    butter
½ teaspoon cumin seeds
1 large red onion, finely chopped
2.5cm piece of ginger, finely chopped
3 green chillies, finely chopped
½ teaspoon red chilli powder
½ teaspoon ground turmeric
1½ teaspoons salt
2 tomatoes, deseeded and finely diced
1 tablespoon butter (optional, to
    finish)
2 tablespoons chopped coriander

Break the eggs into a mixing bowl and whisk lightly.

Heat the oil in a large, heavy-based pan. Add the cumin seeds and let them crackle, then add the onion and sauté over a medium heat for 2–3 minutes until it starts changing colour. Add the ginger and green chillies and stir for 30 seconds.

Add the chilli powder, turmeric and salt and stir quickly to mix thoroughly without burning the spices. Now add the tomatoes and the whisked eggs and stir continually with a wooden spatula or a flat spoon for 3–4 minutes or until the eggs are softly scrambled and the spices are mixed through evenly. You may stir through the additional butter at the end, if you wish, then sprinkle with the chopped coriander.

Serve it with tawa paratha or any grilled flat bread, in a pitta pocket, or even sandwiched in a brioche!

TO START THE DAY

SPICED LAMB MINCE WITH SCRAMBLED EGGS

Known as *kheema gotala*, this is a Bombay café classic. Prepare a classic onion tomato masala for cooking mince, and then finish it with tomato ketchup and egg to make a delicious spicy scrambled filling for breakfast rolls. Alternatively, you can use the mixture between two slices of bread and make a toastie!

SERVES 4

3 tablespoons vegetable oil
2 onions, finely chopped
1 tablespoon Ginger and Garlic Paste (see page 226)
5 green chillies, chopped
2 tomatoes, finely chopped
½ teaspoon ground turmeric
2 teaspoons red chilli powder
2 teaspoons ground coriander
1 teaspoon ground cumin
1 teaspoon garam masala
1 teaspoon salt
500g lamb mince
4 eggs
3 tablespoons tomato ketchup
juice of ½ lime
2–3 tablespoons chopped coriander and mint (roughly equal quantities of each herb)

To serve
4 soft rolls, buttered
1 red onion, chopped
1 green chilli, chopped
2 tablespoons chopped coriander

Heat a heavy-based frying pan and add the oil. When oil is hot, add the onions and cook over a high heat for 6–8 minutes until they turn golden brown, then add the ginger and garlic paste and green chillies and fry gently for 2–3 minutes, stirring well to prevent them sticking to the pan.

Add the tomatoes, dried spices and salt and cook for 3–4 minutes until the liquid from the tomatoes is absorbed and the oil begins to separate from the edges of the masala.

Reduce the heat to very low and add the mince. Work it in well with a spatula until it is totally broken up and thoroughly blended into the masala. Increase the heat to medium and cook, stirring regularly, for 7–8 minutes until the mince is cooked.

Beat the eggs and add them to the hot mince. Stir gently over the heat until they are scrambled to your liking – I like mine very soft as this makes for a great filling. Remove the pan from the heat, add the tomato ketchup and mix well. Check the seasoning, then stir in the lime juice, chopped coriander and mint.

Serve in buttered rolls with the raw onion, chilli and coriander to taste. Alternatively, use the mince as a filling and make a toastie. Either way it tastes superb.

SAVOURY INDIAN PANCAKES

Pancakes, but not as you know them! Called *cheela*, these are savoury, spicy and make a very simple breakfast recipe. We often find ourselves having these when we have friends or relatives staying over. We all have a go at this now and again, but no one really makes these as well as Anisha, my lovely sister-in-law. This is her recipe – do give these a go.

SERVES 4
(2 PANCAKES PER PERSON)

400g coarse semolina (or chickpea flour)
1 tablespoon roasted cumin seeds
4 green chillies, finely chopped
2 red onions, finely chopped
5cm piece of ginger, finely chopped
2 tablespoons chopped coriander
1 tablespoon salt
3 tablespoons vegetable oil
Chaat Masala (see page 224)
Green Coconut Chutney (see page 190) or artichoke podimas (see page 178), to serve as side or filling (optional)

Mix together the semolina, cumin, chillies, onions, ginger, coriander and salt with 700ml water and allow the batter to rest for 15 minutes.

Heat a non-stick frying pan and drizzle with oil. Spoon a ladleful of batter into the pan, spreading it out with the back of the ladle as much as you can. Drizzle with more oil and cook over a high heat for 3–4 minutes until the pancake is crisp and easily comes off the pan base, then turn over and cook another minute or so on the second side.

Sprinkle the pancake with chaat masala and serve with chutney of your choice.

KADHAI-SPICED MUSHROOMS ON TOAST

This dish was inspired by a trip to Bordeaux at a time when ceps were just coming into season. I ordered these delicious crunchy ceps cooked in butter, garlic, parsley and lemon juice, and was reminded of a simple potato dish my mum makes with sliced potatoes, chilli, turmeric and fresh coriander leaves. At Cinnamon Soho I've combined the two different dishes, using king oyster or large shiitake mushrooms, or the eryngi mushroom (otherwise known as chicken-feet mushrooms), but you can use any meaty variety you can lay your hands on. Add a fried or poached egg for a substantial brunch for two.

SERVES 4

4 slices of good-quality bread
1 tablespoon vegetable or corn oil
400g king oyster or similar meaty, chunky mushrooms, cleaned and sliced 7.5mm thick
1 red onion, finely chopped
2.5cm piece of ginger, peeled and finely chopped
2 green chillies, slit and finely chopped
2 tomatoes, deseeded and chopped into 1cm dice
½ teaspoon salt
a pinch of sugar
1 tablespoon butter (optional), plus extra for spreading on the toast
juice of ½ lemon
1 tablespoon chopped coriander stems or leaves

For the kadhai spice crust
1 teaspoon cumin seeds
1 teaspoon coriander seeds
½ teaspoon chilli flakes
¼ teaspoon black peppercorns
2 teaspoons fennel seeds

To make the kadhai spice crust, roast everything in a dry pan for 30–60 seconds until aromatic, then cool and grind coarsely to obtain a spice crust. You will need 1 teaspoon of this mixture for this recipe. The rest can be stored in an airtight container.

Toast the bread and spread with butter (olive oil or pesto also work well).

Heat the oil in a large frying pan until very hot. Spread the sliced mushrooms in the pan and allow to caramelise over a very high heat – this will take 60–90 seconds. Do not move the mushrooms too much until they form a caramelised crust.

Add the onion and stir it in the pan, cook for a minute, then add the ginger and chillies, tomatoes, spice crust, salt and sugar and stir for another minute over a high heat. Stir through the butter and lemon juice to finish, allowing the butter to melt and mix. Mix in the coriander and serve immediately on the toasted bread.

CHORIZO AND CUMIN POTATOES

This is a great example of the kind of cooking that goes on in my home these days. Drawing influences from different parts of the world, whether it's my love for smoky sweet chorizo or the memory of crisp slivers of potatoes with cumin that I so loved as a child. Here it all comes together in one pan. Add a fried egg or two on top and it becomes a truly hearty breakfast!

SERVES 4

4 large Desiree, Maris Piper or any other floury potatoes (750–800g), peeled and sliced into 5mm discs
2 teaspoons salt
½ teaspoon ground turmeric
3 tablespoons vegetable oil
1 teaspoon cumin seeds
½ teaspoon chilli powder
1 teaspoon ground cumin
a pinch of sea salt flakes
2 red onions, sliced into rings 2–3 mm thick
150g cooking chorizo, sliced 5mm thick
1cm piece of ginger, finely chopped
2 green chillies, finely chopped
25g coriander leaves, chopped
2 eggs per person (optional)

First blanch the sliced potatoes. Place them in 500ml boiling water with the salt and half the turmeric for 2–3 minutes, then drain and leave aside.

Heat the oil in a non-stick pan; add the cumin seeds and when they start to crackle, add the potatoes. Cook for a minute or so over a high heat until they begin to colour slightly. Stir to mix and colour evenly as far as possible for another minute or so.

Now add the remaining turmeric, the chilli powder, ground cumin and sea salt flakes. You may need to sprinkle some water over the pan if the spices look as though they may burn.

Add the onion rings and chorizo slices and stir quickly. When the onion starts to soften and the chorizo is heated through, around 2–3 minutes, sprinkle in the ginger, chillies and coriander. Cook for a minute or so until the onion rings are starting to wilt and the potatoes are mostly crisp.

Serve immediately as a hearty brunch on its own or with a fried egg or two per person.

CURRY LEAF SEMOLINA

Semolina upma is one of the most common breakfast dishes in most households in the southern half of the country, but it is rarely seen in hotels or restaurants. It makes for a quick and relatively simple breakfast and you can add vegetables, such as carrots, peas, beans or anything you like, for additional texture.

SERVES 4-6

4 tablespoons vegetable oil
1 teaspoon black mustard seeds
10 curry leaves
2 red onions, finely chopped
2.5cm piece of ginger, finely chopped
3 green chillies, slit lengthways
1½ teaspoons salt
100g vegetables, such as carrots, cauliflower, beans (all chopped into 5mm dice) or peas, or a mixture (optional)
200g coarse semolina or couscous
400ml boiling water
2 teaspoons chopped sun-dried tomatoes
juice of ½ lemon
2 tablespoons chopped coriander

Heat the olive oil in a deep pan. Add the mustard seeds and when they pop, add the curry leaves and onion and sauté for 5–6 minutes until the onion turns translucent. Add the ginger, chillies and salt and stir for a minute or so over a high heat. If you choose to add additional vegetables, now is the time to add them too.

Add the semolina to the pan and cook over medium heat for 4–5 minutes, stirring constantly to prevent it catching on the base of the pan, until the semolina is slightly roasted – you can smell the aroma and the texture resembles that of sand.

Add the boiling water to the pan of semolina and stir to mix evenly. Reduce the heat and cover the pan with a lid. Cook it for 2 minutes, then remove the lid and stir. Add chopped sun-dried tomatoes, cover again and cook for 2–3 minutes until the liquid is absorbed.

Finish with a squeeze of lemon juice and stir through the chopped coriander leaves. Serve either on its own or with green chutney or curried yoghurt as an accompaniment.

DUCK EGG CURRY WITH LAYERED PARATHAS

This *deem* curry is a breakfast like no other! I like to use duck's eggs for their flavour (but you could make this just as well with regular eggs), and suggest keeping the yolk quite runny. When cut through, the runny yolk adds a silky texture which you can mop up using the layered bread. It may seem like a lot of work for breakfast, but it's worth it, especially for a weekend brunch.

SERVES 4

For the eggs
8 duck eggs
vegetable oil, for shallow frying
a pinch of salt
a pinch of ground turmeric

For the sauce
4 tablespoons vegetable oil
4 cloves
2 bay leaves
3 onions, finely chopped
2.5cm piece of ginger, grated
5 garlic cloves, chopped
½ teaspoon ground turmeric
1½ teaspoons red chilli powder
2 teaspoons ground cumin
1 teaspoon salt
6 large ripe tomatoes, puréed
250ml chicken stock or water
2 green chillies, finely chopped
1 teaspoon garam masala
a pinch of sugar
2 tablespoons chopped coriander

To boil the eggs, place in a large pan of cold water and bring to the boil, then reduce to a simmer. Cook for exactly 5½ minutes. The white will be just set and the yolk will be creamy. Dip the eggs immediately in cold water, then carefully peel and keep aside.

Heat the oil for frying in a heavy-based pan, gently add the eggs to the moderately hot pan, add the salt and turmeric and continue to cook over a medium heat, turning the eggs to colour them evenly on all sides. When coloured all over, remove the eggs from the pan with a slotted spoon and drain on kitchen paper.

To make the sauce, heat the oil in the same pan over a high heat, add the cloves and bay leaves and let them pop and release their flavours in the oil. Then add the chopped onions and sauté for 5–6 minutes until golden in colour. Add the ginger and garlic and sauté for 2–3 minutes. Add the turmeric, chilli powder, cumin and salt, stir for a minute to mix well, then add the puréed tomatoes and cook well over a medium heat for 10–12 minutes until the oil begins to separate from the masala.

Add the stock or water to the cooking spices. Mix well and cook for 2–3 minutes. Add the green chillies and garam masala, reduce the heat and simmer for 2 minutes. Finish by stirring in the sugar and checking the seasoning.

Add the prepared eggs to the gravy and fold in very gently to coat on all sides. Garnish with chopped fresh coriander. Serve hot with layered parathas (see page 171).

STUFFED PARATHAS

This is a popular Punjabi breakfast. Dip the bread into yoghurt or pickle if you are more adventurous. Each filling will be enough for 12 parathas.

SERVES 6

550g chapatti flour
1 teaspoon salt
25ml vegetable oil
3 tablespoons ghee, for cooking the parathas

To serve
200ml plain Greek yoghurt
1 teaspoon salt
1 teaspoon sugar
1 teaspoon roasted cumin seeds, ground
50g cold salted butter

Mix together the flour, salt, oil and 225ml water to make a stiff dough. Rest for 15 minutes. Meanwhile, make your chosen filling (see below).

Divide the dough into 12 equal portions and do the same with your chosen filling.

Take a ball of dough, make an indent in the centre with your thumb and keep pressing and rotating the dough in your hand to make the cavity slightly larger than the size of the ball of stuffing. The edges of the cavity of dough should be slightly thinner than the rest of it. Sit the ball of filling in the cavity and bring together the edges to cover it on all sides. Do not leave any cracks or the filling will come out while rolling the parathas.

Lightly dust with flour, gently flatten, then roll out into a pizza 20cm in diameter. Heat a heavy-based frying pan, preferably iron, over a medium-low heat and put a rolled-out paratha on it. Cook for about 2–3 minutes on one side, then flip over and cook the other side for another 2–3 minutes. When both sides become dry and start to colour, brush with a little ghee to get an even colouring and transfer to a foil-lined plate. While this first paratha is cooking, prepare the next one, and so on. Keep the pile of parathas warm by loosely wrapping in foil.

Serve with plain Greek yoghurt which has been lightly salted and thinned slightly with water, sugar and ground roasted cumin seeds and chutney (see pages 190–195). Alternatively, they can also be served with cold salted butter!

For the potato filling
500g Desiree potatoes
5 green chillies, finely chopped
2.5cm piece of ginger, finely chopped
50g coriander, finely chopped
1 red onion, finely chopped
1½ teaspoons carom seeds
1½ teaspoons red chilli powder
1½ teaspoons salt

Peel and boil the potatoes until tender. Drain and allow to cool, then grate using the coarse side of a box grater. Mix all ingredients together and use to fill the paratha.

For the cauliflower filling
1 head of cauliflower (around 750g), grated using the coarse side of a box grater, discarding any stem or hard woody bits
1 tablespoon salt
2 red onions, finely chopped
2.5cm piece of ginger, finely chopped
4 green chillies, finely chopped
50g coriander, finely chopped
1 teaspoon black onion seeds
Sprinkle the grated cauliflower with salt and set aside for 15–20 minutes. Transfer the salted cauliflower into a thin muslin cloth and squeeze to remove excess liquid. Mix the remaining ingredients into the squeezed cauliflower and use to fill the paratha.

For the broccoli filling
1 large head of broccoli (around 750g), grated using the coarse side of a box grater, discarding any stem or hard woody bits
1 tablespoon salt
2 red onions, finely chopped
2.5cm piece of ginger, finely chopped
4 green chillies, finely chopped
10g chopped thyme
50g Parmesan cheese, grated
50g chopped almonds

Sprinkle the grated broccoli with salt and set aside for 15–20 minutes. Transfer the salted broccoli into a thin muslin cloth and squeeze to remove excess liquid. Mix the remaining ingredients into the squeezed broccoli and use to fill the paratha.

For the mooli/white radish filling
3 moolis (around 750g), grated using the coarse side of a box grater, discarding any stem or hard woody bits
1 tablespoon salt
2 red onions, finely chopped
2.5cm piece of ginger, finely chopped
4 green chillies, finely chopped
50g coriander, finely chopped
1 teaspoon black onion seeds

Sprinkle the grated mooli with salt and set aside for 15–20 minutes. Transfer the salted mooli into a thin muslin cloth and squeeze to remove excess liquid. Mix the remaining ingredients into the squeezed mooli and use to fill the paratha.

UTTAPAM WITH CHUTNEY

Also referred to as rice flour pizzas, it was the southern Indians who first popularised this simple dish. As with pizza, half the fun is to be had with experimenting with your own toppings. You can make yours with ham, bacon, sausage or egg if you like, but my favourite is with chopped tomatoes and green chillies.

It was a long time ago but I remember distinctly when travelling as a family through all of south India in 1982. We ate *idlis*, *dosas* and *sambhar* for most of the trip through Andhra Pradesh, Tamil Nadu, Karnataka, all the way until we arrived in Trivandrum, Kerala. I would just not eat anything as it was all cooked in coconut oil! Trying to ask the cook to use any other oil would have been futile as we didn't speak a word of Malayalam and they didn't speak any English or Hindi! My dad parked us all at the shack, then walked to a grocer to buy some regular vegetable oil and brought it back, requesting the chef to cook with it. Thankfully he obliged, and we all had a great meal of freshly made uttapams with sambhar and chutney.

Nowadays uttapams and dosas are popular all over the country and are often sold on the street. You can get chola bhatura and chilli paneer almost anywhere in the south. Uttapams remain a firm favourite

of mine, pretty much anytime of the day but are excellent for breakfast. Making the batter from scratch is a little time consuming and messy but it is easy enough and can be done the night before. Alternatively, make a trip to your local Asian shop and ask for a packet of Gits or order online.

SERVES 4-6

400g packet of dosa mix (available from Asian shops) or see batter recipe below
1 tablespoon vegetable or corn oil
1 red onion, finely chopped
1 yellow pepper, finely diced (optional)
2 tomatoes, skinned, deseeded and finely diced
2 tablespoons finely chopped coriander
4 hot green chillies, finely chopped
Green Coconut Chutney (see page 190) and Sambhar (see page 186), to serve

For the batter (if not using a packet of dosa mix)
80g rice
20g white urad lentils
a pinch of fenugreek seeds

Make up the dosa mix according to the instructions on the packet. It will need time to ferment, so make sure you read the instructions in advance and allow enough time.

Alternatively, if making the batter from scratch, soak the rice, lentils and fenugreek seeds in plenty water for an hour or so, then drain the water, and make a batter using a pestle and mortar and adding approximately 40ml water to grind. Grind to a smooth paste, then leave to rest in a warm space for 4–6 hours or overnight until the batter begins to ferment and rise.

To cook the pancakes, spread a little oil over a large, heavy-based frying pan or a flat griddle and place over a medium heat. Pour 2–3 tablespoons of the batter into the centre of the pan and, using the back of a ladle, spread it out quickly with an outward circular motion to form a pancake about 10cm in diameter.

Dot the edges of the pancake with a little oil and sprinkle with some of the chopped vegetables and coriander to form a colourful topping. Cook over a low heat for about 4 minutes, until golden underneath. Carefully turn over and cook the other side for another 3–4 minutes. Repeat with the remaining batter to make 12–14 pancakes altogether. Serve with the green coconut chutney and sambhar.

TO START THE DAY

THE MIDDLE OF THE DAY

BANGLA SCOTCH EGGS

The Bengalis like savoury cakes – they make them with potatoes and with fish, but call them 'chops'. Here I have given the same treatment to a mixture of vegetables, where the colour of the beetroot gives these a distinctive look.

MAKES 8

18 quail's eggs or 8 regular free-range eggs, soft boiled
50g ghee or clarified butter
½ teaspoon black onion seeds
½ teaspoon fennel seeds
½ teaspoon cumin seeds
3 bay leaves
2 onions, finely chopped
2 carrots, finely chopped
¼ of a medium cauliflower, finely chopped
100g French beans, finely chopped
1 teaspoon red chilli powder
1 teaspoon ground cumin
1 beetroot, boiled, peeled and finely chopped
10g raisins
1 teaspoon salt
½ teaspoon sugar
2 potatoes, boiled, cooled and grated
corn or vegetable oil, for frying

For the spice mix
1 teaspoon roasted coriander seeds
2 green cardamom pods

For crumbing
2 eggs, whisked
150g dried breadcrumbs

If using quail's eggs, place the eggs in a pan with just salted water to cover the eggs and bring to the boil. As soon as the water comes to the boil, keep on the heat for just 45 seconds, then drain and chill the eggs in cold water. Allow to cool completely, then peel the eggs. Keep aside. If using regular eggs, lower the eggs into a pan of boiling salted water and cook for 6 minutes, then drain and chill in cold water.

To make the spice mix, pound the coriander and cardamom seeds coarsely using a pestle and mortar or in a food processor.

Heat the ghee in a deep, heavy-based wok. When hot, add the onion seeds, fennel seeds, cumin seeds and bay leaves. When they begin to crackle, add the onion and sauté for 6–8 minutes, until golden brown.

Now add all the vegetables, apart from the beetroot and the grated potato, as per the order of ingredients and sauté over a medium heat for a total of 4–6 minutes. Then add the red chilli powder, spice mix and the ground cumin and stir for an additional 5 minutes.

Add the raisins and diced beetroot and cook for another minute. Add the salt and sugar and stir well, then add in the grated potato and cook for 3–4 minutes until the mixture is evenly mixed, the colour turns reddish and the mixture becomes slightly shiny due to the ghee.

Cool the mixture, and when cold divide into 8 equal portions (or 18 portions if using quail's eggs). Roll them around the cooled boiled eggs. Dip the balls in the whisked egg, then roll in the dried breadcrumbs. Let the coated eggs cool in the refrigerator before frying.

Deep fry the eggs in batches at 170ºC for 6–8 minutes until golden brown. Drain on kitchen paper. Serve hot with any mustard-based sauce mixed with tomato ketchup.

THE MIDDLE OF THE DAY

BOMBAY CHUTNEY SANDWICH

If you like white bread, there are few better ways to enjoy a white-bread sandwich than this triple decker. Fresh, colourful and filling, it's an all-time Bombay favourite! If you wish, you can also add a layer of mild Cheddar cheese.

SERVES 4

1 teaspoon Chaat Masala
   (see page 224)
½ teaspoon red chilli powder
½ teaspoon ground cumin
12 slices white bread
40g butter, softened
6 tablespoons Green Coriander
   Chutney (see page 190)
250g new potatoes, boiled in the skin,
   peeled and sliced 2.5mm thick
½ cucumber, peeled and sliced 2.5mm
   thick
2 beetroot, boiled, peeled and sliced
   2.5mm thick
50g chopped coriander
50g crisp chickpea vermicelli
   (optional)

Mix together the chaat masala, chilli powder and ground cumin.

Butter a slice of bread on one side. Spread with ½ tablespoon of the coriander chutney, then add a layer of sliced potatoes and sprinkle with the mixed spice seasoning. Top with a layer of cucumber.

Butter another slice of bread on both sides and spread chutney on one side. Place chutney-side down on top of the cucumber layer, then spread more chutney on the top side of the bread. Now add a layer of sliced beetroot, sprinkle with coriander, more spice seasoning and the chickpea vermicelli, if using.

Butter a third slice of bread on one side and place butter-side down on top of the beetroot layer. Cut off the crusts if you wish, and cut the sandwich into halves or quarters. Repeat to make another three sandwiches.

GRILLED CHILLI CHICKEN TOASTIE

This has got to be my favourite midnight snack of all time! When I was training in New Delhi in the 1990s I often used to find myself down to the last 20 rupees in my pocket, and the toss up was between petrol for the scooter, a late-night movie show or dinner. Even the most creative student couldn't manage all three with 20 rupees. My solution was to put 10 rupees of petrol in my scooter, and spend the remaining money on the movie ticket. After the show, I'd drive up to The Oberoi New Delhi's coffee-shop kitchen and volunteer to make their French fries in exchange for a mega grilled sandwich and the largest glass ever of iced coffee! This recipe therefore goes out to the Palms' night-shift team.

SERVES 4

150g cooked Chicken Tikka, chopped
    into 5mm dice (see page 52)
4 green chillies, finely chopped
1 red onion, finely chopped
40g mature Cheddar cheese, chopped
    into 5mm dice
8 slices of good-quality wholemeal,
    multi-grain or brown bread
50g butter, softened
4 tablespoons Green Coriander
    Chutney (see page 190)
salt and pepper

Mix together the chopped chicken, chillies, onion and cheese, and season with salt and pepper.

Lay the bread on a work surface and spread one side of each slice with butter. Spread the green chutney on four slices only. Divide the filling between the four chutney slices, then cover with the remaining slices.

Place in a sandwich toaster and cook until golden and crisp on the outside and the cheese melts inside. If you don't have a sandwich toaster, simply griddle for a couple of minutes on each side. Cut and serve with tomato ketchup or chutney of your choice.

THE MIDDLE OF THE DAY

CHILLI AND CHEESE TOAST

These were very popular in the college canteen in Delhi, especially when it was my turn to service the fast-food café. Before I joined the college, they would use white sliced bread and a mix of paneer, peppers and any nondescript cheese. When I ran the shift, I would often up the chilli and serve stronger cheese and crustier bread. All very controversial in the beginning, but it turned out to be a very popular move in the end!

SERVES 4

8 thick slices of rye or sourdough bread (or any multi-grain, farmhouse-type bread)
6 green chillies, finely chopped
2.5cm piece of ginger, finely chopped
2 tablespoons olive oil
pinch of sea salt flakes
250g mature Cheddar cheese, sliced thinly
½ teaspoon cracked black peppercorns
1 tablespoon finely chopped coriander
Worcestershire sauce

Toast the bread. Mix together the chillies, ginger, oil and salt and spread on to the toast. Arrange the cheese slices on top and bake under the grill for 2–3 minutes, until the cheese is melted.

Remove from the grill, sprinkle with cracked pepper and coriander and drizzle with Worcestershire sauce.

Tip
You may wish to use a mixture of different cheeses and/or add some finely chopped red onion to the cheeses – it's entirely up to you!

CREAMY CHICKEN FOCACCIA SANDWICH

This subtly flavoured dish is easy to prepare. Here it's worth looking out for better quality poultry – organic and corn-fed birds often lose their distinctive tastes when given the spice treatment, but aromatic spices like mace and cardamom will help justify the extra expense.

SERVES 4

4 chicken breasts, skinned and each
    cut into 4–5 pieces
focaccia bread or similar flatbread to
    make 4 sandwiches
4 tablespoons Green Coriander
    Chutney (see page 190)
a handful of rocket leaves
juice of 1 lime

For the first marinade
1 teaspoon salt
1 tablespoon Ginger and Garlic Paste
    (see page 226)

For the second marinade
2 tablespoons cream cheese
1 tablespoon Greek yoghurt
1cm piece of ginger, finely chopped
2 large green chillies, finely chopped
a pinch of ground mace
a pinch of ground cardamom
½ teaspoon salt
¼ teaspoon ground white pepper
2 tablespoons single cream
1 tablespoon chopped basil (or basil
    pesto)

Place six wooden skewers in a bowl of water to soak.

Marinate the chicken breast with salt and ginger and garlic paste and set aside for 20 minutes.

For the second marinade, break the cheese into a mixing bowl. Stir in the yoghurt to form a smooth paste, then add the ginger, chillies, mace, cardamom, salt and pepper. Fold in the cream and the basil or pesto (do this carefully as this mixture might split if mixed vigorously). Apply this second marinade to the chicken and set aside in the fridge for another 20 minutes before cooking.

Preheat oven to 200ºC/Gas Mark 6.

Remove the chicken from the marinade and thread onto the pre-soaked bamboo skewers. Place on a baking tray and cook in the preheated oven for 10–15 minutes.

In the meantime, warm the bread and smear with the green chutney.

Top the bread with the cooked chicken and any juices. Sprinkle with rocket, squeeze the lime juice over, cover and serve as a juicy, fresh sandwich like no other.

PULLED LAMB WRAP

This is a great way to use up any *raan* left over from the recipe on page 165. It's great as a filling for naan bread, but works just as well wrapped in a tortilla. I like the filling to be warm so I stir-fry the pulled meat with sliced onions, pepper, carrots or other veggies, but if you don't feel like cooking, simply mix together the shredded veggies as a salad with pulled lamb and some mayo and enjoy it cold.

This is a great fist-food option for a working lunch, and it's a particular favourite lunch of ours while shooting the photographs for our cookbooks.

SERVES 4

4 naan bread (see page 169)
2 tablespoons vegetable oil
1 red onion, thinly sliced
½ green pepper, cut into thin matchsticks
1 carrot, cut into thin matchsticks
1 green chilli, finely chopped
½ teaspoon salt
250g pulled lamb, from leftover *raan* (see page 165)
1 tablespoon tomato ketchup
a pinch of Chaat Masala (see page 224)
1 tablespoon chopped coriander
4 tablespoons Green Coriander Chutney (see page 190)
2 tablespoons mayonnaise (optional)
juice of ½ lemon

Preheat oven to 120°C/Gas mark ½. Cut four pieces of greaseproof paper, large enough to hold the wraps.

Place the naan bread in the oven to warm for 3–4 minutes.

Meanwhile, heat the oil in a frying pan, add the red onion and pepper and sauté for 2–3 minutes over a high heat until the vegetables are slightly coloured but retaining their crunch. Add the carrot, green chilli, salt and lamb and stir-fry over a high heat for 1–2 minutes until the lamb is warm. Then add the ketchup, chaat masala and coriander and stir briskly for another minute.

Place the warmed naans on the greaseproof paper. Divide the filling equally between the four naans. Drizzle over the coriander chutney and mayo, if using, and squeeze the lemon over all the pieces. Roll the naan up like a wrap, so that it is sealed at the base and open at the top. Wrap in the greaseproof paper and serve immediately.

ASPARAGUS WITH CURRIED YOGHURT AND GUNPOWDER

When asparagus is tender and in season, you don't need to peel. Simply snap the spears and from the point where they break, they're good to eat. The stems and trims can be used to make a soup or stir-fry. The gunpowder refers to a Dry Lentil Chutney (see page 192) served alongside the asparagus originally from south India. It adds crunch and firepower to the dish – gunpowder indeed!

SERVES 4

2 tablespoons vegetable or corn oil
24 green asparagus spears, trimmed from the bottom and peeled if necessary
½ teaspoon salt
1 teaspoon butter
1 tablespoon chopped coriander
juice of ½ a lemon
Dry Lentil Chutney (see page 192), to serve
Curried Yoghurt (see page 225), to serve

For the kadhai spices
1 teaspoon fennel seeds
1 teaspoon cumin seeds
½ teaspoon coriander seeds
2 whole red chillies

To prepare the kadhai spices, dry roast all the seeds and the chillies in a pan over a medium heat for a few minutes until they smell aromatic. Allow to cool, then pound to make a coarse mixture.

Preheat the grill. Heat the oil in a heavy-based pan, add the asparagus and sear on each side for about 1 minute, sprinkling over the salt during cooking. Remove the pan from the heat, add the butter and the kadhai spices. Place the pan under a hot grill for a further minute, until the asparagus are soft. Sprinkle with the chopped coriander and the lemon juice.

Serve the asparagus hot, with the curried yoghurt alongside and dry lentil chutney.

HOMELY BLACK LENTILS

Black lentils, or *dal makhani*, are a firm favourite in all our restaurants, and rightly so. They're so unctuous and rich when cooked with cream, butter and tomatoes! This is a slightly different version, more often found in homes in Punjab. It's a rather rough and ready version fondly referred to as *Ma Ki Dal* (Mum's Lentils) since it is wholesome and delicious!

SERVES 4

150g split urad dal (black lentils)
2 large onions, thinly sliced
2 green chillies, slit lengthwise
a pinch of asafoetida
4 tablespoons vegetable oil or ghee
1 teaspoon cumin seeds
5cm piece of ginger, cut into fine matchsticks
3 cloves garlic, finely chopped
2 large tomatoes, diced
1 tablespoon ground coriander
1 teaspoon ground cumin
1½ teaspoons salt
1 teaspoon red chilli powder
75ml double cream, lightly whisked

Soak the black lentils in a bowl of water for 2 hours, or overnight if possible.

Drain the lentils, then place in a pan with half the onion, green chillies, half the asafoetida and salt to taste. Add 1.5 litres of water, bring to the boil and cook for 30–40 minutes until they are very tender and completely disintegrated.

In a separate pan, heat the oil and add cumin seeds and remaining asafoetida, stir for 30 seconds or so until the seeds start to crackle, then add the remaining onion and fry for about 10 minutes over a medium heat until golden. Add the ginger and garlic and fry for a minute. Add the tomatoes, coriander, ground cumin, salt and red chilli powder and fry for another 5 minutes.

Add the boiled lentil mixture and enough additional water, if required, to make a thick gravy-like consistency and mix well. Simmer for 10 minutes.

Pour in the whisked cream and mix well. Remove from the heat, check the seasoning and serve with naan bread or paratha of your choice (see pages 168–171).

PUNJABI RAJMA MASALA

This recipe is yet another one of the hundreds of possibilities that lentils, pulses and beans present in Indian food. Neither my wife, Archana, nor I are from Punjab, but somehow *Rajma-chawal* (kidney bean curry and steamed rice) has made it to the top of the charts in the Singh household.

SERVES 4

100g red kidney beans, soaked overnight (alternatively use tinned kidney beans)
3 tablespoons vegetable oil
2 bay leaves
2 onions, finely chopped
2.5cm piece of ginger, finely chopped
6–8 garlic cloves, finely chopped
2 teaspoons red chilli powder
1 tablespoon ground coriander
½ teaspoon ground turmeric
1 teaspoon ground cumin
4 tomatoes, chopped
1 teaspoon salt, or to taste
1 teaspoon dried fenugreek leaves, crushed lightly
1 teaspoon garam masala
1 tablespoon chopped coriander

Pressure-cook the kidney beans with five cups of water until you hear five whistles or until totally cooked and soft. If you don't have a pressure cooker, place the kidney beans in a pan, cover with 2 litres of cold water, bring to the boil and boil vigorously for 10 minutes. Lower the heat, cover and simmer for 1½–2 hours or until tender. Alternatively, use tinned kidney beans which do not require any pre-cooking and can be used straight from the tin.

Heat the oil in a deep pan. Add the bay leaves and onions and sauté for 6–8 minutes until golden. Add the ginger and garlic and continue to sauté for a minute. Add the chilli, ground coriander, turmeric and cumin and stir, then add the tomatoes and salt and cook for about 5 minutes until the tomatoes are cooked and the oil begins to leave the masala.

Add the cooked kidney beans along with the cooking liquid (or all the liquid in the tin, if using tinned beans) and mix together. Cook over a low heat for 15 minutes, stirring occasionally. Adjust the salt, add the dried fenugreek leaves and garam masala and cook for 2 minutes. Garnish with coriander leaves and serve hot with steamed rice.

CHICKEN TIKKA

Tandoori-spiced chicken tikka is possibly one of the most versatile components you could have in your fridge. Great as a snack or starter on its own, or as an addition to salads, a filler for lunchtime wraps or chopped as a sandwich filling, the options are endless. This is a very simple recipe for chicken tikka which uses boneless chicken thighs. You could use breast meat if you prefer, but thighs are the real deal and have a much better flavour.

SERVES 4

600g boneless and skinless chicken thighs, each thigh cut into two
Chaat Masala (see page 224) to garnish
juice of ½ lemon
8 bamboo skewers, soaked in water overnight or a couple of hours

For the marinade
2 tablespoons Ginger and Garlic Paste (see page 226)
juice of ½ lemon
1½ teaspoons red chilli powder
1 teaspoon salt

For the flavoured yoghurt
100ml plain yoghurt
1 teaspoon red chilli powder
1 teaspoon cumin seeds
½ teaspoon garam masala
½ teaspoon salt
1 tablespoon chopped coriander
2 tablespoons vegetable oil

Mix the marinade ingredients together in a bowl, add the chicken and set aside for 10 minutes.

In the meantime, mix together all the ingredients for the flavoured yoghurt.

After 10 minutes, mix the chicken thighs and the marinade into the flavoured yoghurt and marinate in the fridge for a couple of hours or preferably overnight. Soak the bamboo skewers in water for the same amount of time.

Preheat oven to 220ºC/Gas Mark 7.

Thread the chicken on to the wooden skewers and place on a wire rack placed over a baking tray. Bake in the preheated oven for 8–12 minutes, turning the skewers after about 8 minutes, then finish for 5–6 minutes under a grill for the charred effect.

Remove from the oven, sprinkle with chaat masala and a squeeze of lemon juice and serve immediately.

MASALA CHICKEN LIVERS ON TOAST

Chicken livers are an acquired taste and people who love them will die for them! You may substitute with duck's livers or even foie gras if you can find some.

SERVES 4

300g chicken livers, trimmed
2 tablespoons vegetable oil
1 teaspoon salt
1 teaspoon red chilli powder
2 green chillies finely chopped
2.5cm piece of ginger, finely chopped
1 teaspoon cumin seeds
2 red onions, finely chopped
1 tomato, finely chopped
juice of ¼ lemon
1 teaspoon chopped coriander
toast, to serve

Marinate the chicken livers in a bowl with half the oil, half the salt, half the chilli powder, the chopped green chillies and chopped ginger. Mix together well and set aside for 20–30 minutes.

Heat the remaining oil in a pan; add the cumin seeds and cook over a medium heat for about 1 minute until they crackle. Add the chopped onions and sauté for 10–12 minutes until golden, then add the remaining chilli powder, tomato and salt. Cook until the onions and tomato are soft, then set aside.

Heat a separate non-stick frying pan over a high heat, add the marinated chicken livers and sear for about 1 minute on each side, making sure they are nicely coloured, then add in the onion and tomato masala and quickly toss the livers in it. Finish with the chopped coriander and lemon juice. Serve on toast.

BARBECUED CHICKEN WITH COCONUT MILK

This is a quick and simple recipe using under fillets of chicken which are extremely tender and quick to cook. These can also be threaded onto pre-soaked bamboo skewers and cooked on a barbecue.

SERVES 4-6
(AS A SNACK)

24 mini fillets of chicken or
    5–6 chicken breasts
2 tablespoons groundnut oil, for
    grilling

For the marinade
zest and juice of 2 limes
50g ginger, grated on a microplane
3 garlic cloves, grated on a microplane
3 green chillies, finely chopped
2 shallots, finely chopped
1 teaspoon salt
1 teaspoon cracked black pepper
250ml coconut milk
25g chives, chopped into 2.5cm
    lengths
1 tablespoon sugar

If using chicken breasts, cut into fine slices.

To make the marinade, mix all the ingredients together in a large bowl, then add the chicken and marinate for 3–4 hours in the fridge.

Cook the chicken on a hot griddle pan for 3–5 minutes, turning to cook on both sides, brushing with any leftover marinade and grilling until cooked through.

POTATO BONDA BURGERS

Have you been to Mumbai, but never had a *vada pao*? If so, you haven't lived. The local trains in Mumbai are the lifeline of the city and this ever-popular street snack is the fuel of its people. Spicy vegetable or potato bombs served inside soft rolls, spiked with fresh green and tangy tomato ketchup, this makes a great change from the meaty burgers we're so used to.

SERVES 4

2 tablespoons vegetable or corn oil
1 teaspoon mustard seeds
½ teaspoon white urad lentils
4 green chillies, chopped
2.5cm piece of ginger, peeled and chopped
10 curry leaves
2 red onions, sliced
½ teaspoon ground turmeric
3 medium potatoes, boiled, peeled and grated (approximately 400–500g grated weight)
juice of ½ lemon
1 tablespoon chopped coriander leaves
1 teaspoon salt
vegetable oil, for deep frying

For the batter
100g gram flour
¼ teaspoon ground turmeric
¼ teaspoon red chilli powder
½ teaspoon salt
a pinch of carom seeds

150ml water,
¼ teaspoon Ginger and Garlic Paste (optional, see page 226)

To serve
4 burger buns
50g salted butter
6 tablespoons Green Coriander Chutney (see page 190)
½ cucumber, sliced
2 tomatoes, sliced
¼ iceberg lettuce
4 tablespoons tomato ketchup (optional)

To make the bonda mix, heat the oil in a heavy-based pan over a high heat. When it is hot, add the mustard seeds, urad dal, green chillies, ginger, curry leaves and onions. Sauté for 3–4 minutes, then add the turmeric and mix well for 1 minute.

Add the grated potatoes, reduce the heat to low and stir well for 5 minutes, then add the lemon juice and coriander leaves. Add the salt, mix well and set aside to cool. When cold, divide into four balls and shape as patties.

Slice the burger buns in half and spread with butter. Heat a pan and sear the cut sides of the buns.

To make the batter, simply whisk all the ingredients together.

Heat the oil in a wok or in a deep-fat fryer to 170ºC. Dip the shaped potato patties in the chickpea batter and deep fry for 3–5 minutes until golden in colour. Remove and drain on kitchen paper.

Spread the chutney on the bottom half of the bun, arrange the cucumber, tomato and lettuce on top and then add the potato patties. Cover with the top of the bun and serve with more green coriander chutney and tomato ketchup on the side.

AUBERGINE FRITTERS WITH POPPY SEEDS

Begun Bhaja (as these thinly sliced long aubergine fritters are known in Bengal) make an excellent accompaniment to a curry meal, but work just as well as snacks with drinks. Feel free to replace the Japanese aubergines with ordinary aubergines or courgettes if you prefer.

SERVES 4
(AS A SNACK)

2 long Japanese aubergines (or courgettes), sliced lengthways 3–4 mm thick, using a mandolin or a sharp knife
2 garlic cloves, finely chopped
1½ teaspoons red chilli powder
1 teaspoon turmeric
1 teaspoon salt
½ teaspoon nigella seeds
1 green chilli, finely chopped
½ teaspoon sugar
1 tablespoon chopped coriander
juice of ½ lemon
3 tablespoons cornflour
2 tablespoons coarse semolina
1 tablespoon poppy seeds
vegetable or corn oil, for deep frying
Chaat Masala (see page 224), to sprinkle

Arrange the aubergine slices on a tray. Sprinkle evenly with the chopped garlic, chilli powder, turmeric, salt, nigella, green chilli, sugar and coriander and squeeze the lemon juice over the aubergines. Turn the slices so that both sides are covered. Set aside for 10–15 minutes.

In the meantime, mix together the cornflour, semolina and poppy seeds and tip on to a wide tray or plate. Taking one aubergine slice at a time, dip in the flour mixture and pat with your fingers to coat evenly and to make the coating stick.

Deep fry in hot oil at 180ºC for 3–4 minutes, a few pieces at a time, until the aubergine is crisp. Remove from the hot oil with a slotted spoon and drain on a plate lined with kitchen paper, then sprinkle with chaat masala and serve hot either with your main meal or as a starter with tomato or coriander chutney.

KICHRI WITH PICKLED CAULIFLOWER AND PEAS

Kedgeree, or *kichri* as it is known in India, is a humble dish perfectly suited to cold, rainy days. When it is combined with sharp, crunchy, caramelised, spicy cauliflower, there is a fascinating interaction of textures and flavours.

SERVES 4

2 tablespoons vegetable or corn oil
1 teaspoon cumin seeds
½ teaspoon black onion seeds
½ teaspoon fennel seeds
2.5cm piece of ginger, finely chopped
3 green finger chillies, slit and finely chopped
½ cauliflower, cut into 1cm florets
½ teaspoon salt
¼ teaspoon sugar
a pinch of ground turmeric
2 tablespoons white wine vinegar or cider vinegar
50g coriander, chopped
150g petit pois or green peas, fresh or frozen
juice of 1 lemon

For the kedgeree
125g split yellow moong lentils
a pinch of turmeric
3 tablespoons ghee or clarified butter
1 teaspoon cumin seeds
4 garlic cloves, finely chopped
1 large onion, chopped
1cm piece of ginger, finely chopped
2 green chillies, finely chopped
1½ teaspoons salt

90g basmati rice (uncooked weight), boiled
2 tablespoons sprouted green moong lentils (see page 226)
1 tomato, deseeded and cut into 1cm dice
2 tablespoons chopped coriander
juice of 1 lemon

To make the kedgeree, rinse the yellow moong lentils, put them in a pan with the turmeric and 500ml water and bring to the boil. Simmer for about 20 minutes, until the lentils are tender and all the water has evaporated. Remove from the heat and set aside.

Heat 2 tablespoons of the ghee or butter in a frying pan, add the cumin seeds and garlic and cook gently for 2–3 minutes until golden. Add the onion and sauté for about 10 minutes until it begins to colour, then stir in the ginger and green chillies and cook for a minute. Stir in the yellow moong lentils and salt, then fold in the cooked rice. Add the sprouted green moong lentils, tomato and fresh coriander and stir over a low heat for 3–4 minutes. Stir through the remaining tablespoon of ghee or butter and the lemon juice. Remove from the heat and keep warm.

To cook the cauliflower, heat the oil in a frying pan, add cumin seeds and let them crackle. Add the onion seeds, fennel seeds, ginger and chilli and then the cauliflower. Stir over a high heat for a minute or two, then add the salt, sugar, turmeric, vinegar and 2 tablespoons of water. Stir to mix, then cover with a lid, reduce the heat and allow the cauliflower to cook in its own steam for 2–3 minutes.

Remove the lid, add the coriander and peas and heat through. Divide the kedgeree between four plates and serve with the cauliflower stir-fry on top.

BENGALI KICHRI WITH DRIED PRAWNS

I remember my Dad used to say a true Bengali can't have a single meal without fish or something fishy! *Kichri* – a form of kedgeree – was something that was made every Saturday for lunch and even more of a fixture if it happened to be a rainy or even overcast day. Variations of this dish would include a vegetarian version with peas, cauliflower, carrots and so on, a plain version to be enjoyed with rich spicy mutton curry, and this dried prawn version when there wasn't enough fish to feed the entire family! I use the tiny, strong-smelling dried prawns (or shrimps) – it's easiest to chop these using a food processor.

SERVES 2

150g split yellow mung beans
a pinch of ground turmeric
4 tablespoons ghee or clarified butter
1 teaspoon cumin seeds
6 garlic cloves, finely chopped
1 large onion, chopped
2 tablespoons dried prawns, grounded coarsely
2.5cm piece of fresh ginger, finely chopped
3 hot green finger chillies, finely chopped
1 teaspoon salt
100g boiled basmati rice (30g uncooked weight)
2 tomatoes, deseeded and cut into 1cm dice
2 tablespoons chopped coriander
juice of 1 lemon

To make the kedgeree, wash the split mung beans, place in a pan with 750ml cold water and the turmeric and bring to a boil. Simmer for 25 minutes until the lentils are disintegrated and all the water has evaporated, then remove from the heat and set aside.

Heat the ghee or butter in a pan and add the cumin seeds. When they crackle, add the garlic and onion and sauté over a medium-high heat for 5–8 minutes until they begin to colour. Add the dried prawns, ginger and green chillies and cook for 2 minutes. Stir in the mung beans and salt, then gently fold the rice. Mix in the tomato and half the coriander and stir over a low heat for 3–4 minutes. Finish with the remaining coriander and lemon juice.

CHILLI CARAMEL CASHEW NUT, APPLE AND FENNEL

Inspired by my dear chef friend Eric Chavot's salad Landaise, this is a vegetarian version that is just as brilliant and works well at home. My wife Archana loves it.

SERVES 6

For the croutons
½ baguette
3–4 tablespoons good-quality olive oil

For the chilli cashew nuts
120g whole cashew nuts
1 teaspoon red chilli powder
½ teaspoon salt
50g dark brown sugar
1 egg white, lightly beaten

For the dressing
1 garlic clove, crushed
2 tablespoons honey
2 tablespoons English mustard
40g soured cream
40g mayonnaise
dash of Worcestershire sauce
dash of Tabasco
salt and freshly ground black pepper

For the salad
2 romaine (cos) lettuce, each cut into three pieces
½ bulb of fennel, peeled and thinly sliced using a mandolin
1 Granny Smith, cored and cut into matchsticks
1 red apple, cored and cut into matchsticks
a pinch of crushed chilli flakes
1 tablespoon chopped chives
50g green grapes, sliced
50g black grapes, sliced

To make the croutons, Preheat oven to 160ºC/Gas Mark 3. Slice the baguette 2–3mm thick and arrange the slices on a baking tray in a single layer. Bake in the preheated oven for 3–4 minutes, then drizzle with the olive oil and bake again for 2 minutes or until the croutons are crisp. Allow to cool, then store in an airtight container until required.

To dry-roast the cashews, Preheat oven to 160ºC/Gas Mark 3. Place the cashews on a baking tray and roast for 8–10 minutes. Remove from the oven. Dissolve the chilli powder in 1 tablespoon of water. Mix the cashews with the chilli liquid, salt, sugar and egg white. Mix together well, then spread again on a baking tray lined with greaseproof paper or an oiled tray and bake for a further 6–8 minutes until dried and crisp. Remove from the oven, separate the nuts and let them cool. Store in an airtight container.

To make the dressing, place the ingredients in a blender and blend for 30 seconds until smooth. Taste and season with salt and pepper if required. Keep refrigerated until needed.

Place the lettuce pieces in a bowl of iced water to chill and crisp up for 5 minutes, then drain and pat dry with kitchen paper. Keeping the lettuce in 6 large pieces, sprinkle with salt between the layers.

Toss the fennel and apple with 2 tablespoons of the dressing, sprinkle with chilli flakes and scatter over the chives, croutons, grapes and chilli caramel cashews. Serve immediately.

QUINOA SALAD WITH WATERMELON

This is a dish that we invented by accident but it has worked wonders for us! The unusual combination of chilled watermelon, hoisin and cashew nuts makes it a delectable canapé. The cashews provide a crunchy texture to the succulent watermelon. Add the quinoa and it makes a great light lunch.

SERVES 4

400g watermelon with seeds (peeled weight), cut into 1cm dice
¼ teaspoon red chilli powder
10 fresh mint leaves, chopped
½ teaspoon salt
2 teaspoons sesame seeds
50g lightly salted cashew nuts
juice of ½ lime
3 tablespoons hoisin sauce

For the quinoa salad

2 teaspoons vegetable or corn oil
½ teaspoon mustard seeds
200g quinoa, boiled according to packet instructions
2cm piece of ginger, finely chopped
1 green chilli, finely chopped
1 tablespoon chopped coriander
½ red pepper, thinly sliced
1 teaspoon salt
½ teaspoon sugar
juice of ½ lemon

Combine the watermelon, red chilli powder, mint and salt in a medium sized bowl and refrigerate for 30 minutes. Drain and discard the liquid.

Toast the sesame seeds in a dry pan for 1 minute, then set aside. Toast the cashew nuts in the same way, then halve or chop them and set aside.

Whisk the lime juice and hoisin sauce together in small bowl to blend, then stir in the toasted sesame seeds.

To serve as a canapé, make sure the watermelon is chilled. Sprinkle the hoisin dressing on each cube. Place on a serving tray, sprinkle over the cashew nuts and serve immediately.

To make the quinoa salad, heat the oil in a pan and add the mustard seeds. When they start to crackle, remove from the heat and mix them in a bowl with the quinoa. Mix with the remaining ingredients and adjust the seasoning.

Divide the quinoa between four plates and spoon on the watermelon salad. Top each salad with hoisin dressing, sprinkle with cashew nuts and serve.

THE MIDDLE OF THE DAY

QUINOA AND AUBERGINE KEDGEREE

This is an unusual kedgeree but quite a healthy one, and the sweet and sour flavours of aubergine work well with quinoa. If you wish, garnish with a tahini-flavoured yoghurt *lebne*, and garnish with pomegranate seeds.

SERVES 2

100g quinoa
3 tablespoons vegetable or corn oil
1 whole dried red chilli, broken into three pieces
1 teaspoon mustard seeds
20 curry leaves
1 large onion, finely chopped
1 large aubergine, cut into 1cm dice
1 fresh green chilli, finely chopped
1cm piece of ginger, finely chopped
1 teaspoon salt
2 tablespoons tamarind pulp
¼ teaspoon red chilli powder
½ teaspoon sugar
1 tablespoon finely chopped coriander or basil
juice of ½ lemon

Soak the quinoa in cold water for 15 minutes, then drain and refresh with new water. Bring a pan of approximately 300ml salted water to the boil, add the quinoa and bring back to boil. Reduce to a simmer and cook uncovered for 15–18 minutes or until the grains are cooked but still retain some bite (quinoa develops a white ring on the outer circumference of each grain when it is just about ready). Drain the quinoa through a colander to lose excess moisture.

While the quinoa is cooking, you can start cooking the vegetables. Heat the oil in a heavy-based pan, add whole red chilli and mustard seeds, allow them to crackle and splutter for 30 seconds, then add the curry leaves. The leaves fry in less than a minute – as soon as they are crisp, add the onion and cook for 6–8 minutes or until it starts to turn golden. Now add the diced aubergine, green chillies, ginger and salt and stir for a minute. Reduce the heat, cover with a lid and cook covered for a couple of minutes, then remove the lid, add the tamarind pulp and stir to mix well.

Increase the heat, add the red chilli powder and cook for 10–15 minutes until most of the moisture has dried up and the onion-aubergine mix begins to come together and the aubergine is cooked.

Add the cooked quinoa and mix for a minute or two until heated through. Finish with the sugar, a sprinkling of green coriander or basil and the lemon juice. Mix through and serve hot either on its own or with cooling yoghurt and pomegranate seeds as garnish.

CUCUMBER, PEANUT AND COCONUT SALAD

This is a variation on the Maharashtrian-style *koshimbir* salad which normally uses soaked yellow moong lentils and/or carrots. This version with cucumber is fresh, light and particularly good with grilled meats, fish, barbecues or even as a simple salad.

SERVES 2

For the salad
2 cucumbers, peeled, cored and chopped into 1cm dice
1 teaspoon salt
1 teaspoon sugar
75g roasted peanuts
75g freshly grated coconut
juice of 1 lemon (or more if required)
1 tablespoon chopped coriander
1 tablespoon chopped mint
1–2 green chillies, finely chopped

For the tempering
1 tablespoon vegetable oil
½ teaspoon black mustard seeds
10 curry leaves

Place the cucumber dice on a plate and sprinkle with half salt and sugar. Set aside for 15–20 minutes, then squeeze the water from the cucumber and place the cucumber in a serving bowl.

Using a pestle and mortar, coarsely crush the roasted peanuts. Mix the peanuts, coconut, lemon juice, coriander and mint leaves with the cucumber and the chopped green chillies.

Heat the oil in a pan, add the mustard seeds and fry about 30 seconds or so until they pop, then add the curry leaves and fry for a few seconds. Pour this entire tempering mixture into the bowl of cucumber. Toss well, then chill. Just before serving, add remaining sugar and salt, mix well and serve chilled.

BROCCOLI AND PUFFED RICE SALAD

This is inspired by the Bengali street snack *jhal muri* which is puffed rice with boiled potatoes, chillies, pickle, mustard oil and crisp peanuts, simply tossed together and served as a snack. I remember my parents always discouraged us from having these as they weren't healthy or hygienic, but with my broccoli version, I can see parents changing their tune.

SERVES 2

1 head of broccoli, cut into florets and finely chopped, stems and woody stalk discarded
1 red onion, finely chopped
2 green chillies, finely chopped
1 tablespoon chopped coriander
2.5cm piece of ginger, peeled and finely chopped
1 boiled potato, peeled and chopped into 5mm dice
½ teaspoon red chilli flakes
1½ teaspoons salt
1 teaspoon roasted cumin seeds, ground
1 teaspoon sugar
juice of 2 limes
3 tablespoons mustard or vegetable oil
1 tomato, seeds removed and flesh chopped into 5mm dice
4 tablespoons puffed rice (available from Asian supermarkets)
50g roasted peanuts or cashew nuts, crushed

Mix together all the ingredients, except the puffed rice and nuts, in a large serving bowl. Set aside for 10 minutes.

Just before serving, mix in the puffed rice and nuts and serve.

CAULIFLOWER AND CHICKPEA SALAD WITH WALNUTS AND RAISINS

A vegetarian and gluten-free recipe using different textures of cauliflower – finely chopped cauliflower resembles couscous, while small florets are used as a pickle. Walnuts, raisins and chickpeas all add different textures to the dish.

SERVES 4

1 cauliflower, half cut into 1cm florets for the pickle, half blended to resemble the texture of couscous
12 roasted walnuts
6 pink radishes, thinly sliced using a mandolin
a handful of pea shoots
juice of 1 lemon

For the cauliflower 'couscous'
1 tablespoon vegetable or corn oil
1 tablespoon white wine vinegar
1 tablespoon honey
1 teaspoon salt
freshly ground black pepper
1 tablespoon chopped mint
1 tablespoon chopped coriander

For the pickle
100ml white wine vinegar
½ teaspoon salt
2 tablespoons sugar
a pinch of turmeric
½ teaspoon nigella seeds
1 teaspoon fennel seeds
½ teaspoon dried red chilli flakes
80g tinned chickpeas, drained
40g raisins

For the cauliflower as couscous, core the cauliflower and divide it into florets. Chop finely, either by hand or in a food processor.

To make the 'couscous', heat the oil in a large frying pan or wok. Add the blended cauliflower, vinegar and honey. Season well with salt and pepper. Stir quickly over a medium heat for 3 minutes until the cauliflower is just tender.

To make the pickle, place the vinegar, salt, sugar and spices in a separate pan with 100ml water and bring to the boil, then add the cauliflower florets, chickpeas and raisins. Turn the heat off, cover with a lid and leave to cool down, then chill in the fridge.

To serve, place the 'couscous' in a bowl and stir through the pickled cauliflower and the chopped herbs. Garnish with the roasted walnuts, sliced radishes and pea shoots, and squeeze over the lemon juice.

TANDOORI-STYLE KING PRAWNS AND YOGHURT RICE

I like to use freshwater king prawns as they hold the marinade better and are sweeter and juicier, but seawater prawns work just as well. Serve with a fresh salad of your choice and chilled yoghurt rice on a hot summer's day for the best lunch ever.

SERVES 4

500g headless king prawns, peeled and deveined with tail intact
1 tablespoon vegetable or corn oil

For the yoghurt rice
200g basmati rice
2 green chillies, chopped
2.5cm piece of ginger, finely chopped
2 teaspoons salt
350g plain yoghurt
5 curry leaves, finely chopped
½ carrot, chopped into 5mm dice
½ cucumber, peeled, cored and chopped into 5mm dice
seeds from ¼ pomegranate

For tempering
2 tablespoons vegetable oil
2 whole dried red chillies, broken
1 teaspoon mustard seeds
10 curry leaves
1 red onion, chopped
1 tablespoon chopped coriander

For the first marinade
1 tablespoon ginger-garlic paste
½ teaspoon ground turmeric
1 teaspoon salt
½ teaspoon carom seeds (optional)

For the second marinade
2 tablespoons Greek yoghurt
2 tablespoons cream cheese
2 tablespoons single cream
1cm piece of ginger, finely chopped
1 green chilli, finely chopped
1 tablespoon chopped coriander
1 teaspoon garam masala
2 tablespoons vegetable oil
1 teaspoon salt
juice of 1 lemon

Soak 8 bamboo skewers in water for a couple of hours.

To make the yoghurt rice, boil the rice in a large pan of water for longer than normal, until it is almost overcooked, then drain and allow to cool. Add the green chilli, ginger, salt, yoghurt and curry leaves and mix well. Add the carrots, cucumber and pomegranate seeds and refrigerate to chill.

To temper the rice, heat the oil in a pan and add the dried chilli. When it splutters, smokes and changes colour to dark, add the mustard seeds, curry leaves and onion and cook until the onion turns golden brown. Tip this mixture into the prepared rice and mix in, sprinkle over the coriander leaves and serve chilled.

Place the prawns in a mixing bowl, mix in all the ingredients for the first marinade and set aside for 10 minutes.

Heat the oil in a large heavy-based frying pan, add the prawns and sear quickly so that they curl up. Remove from the heat immediately and set aside to cool.

Preheat oven to 200ºC/Gas Mark 6.

Mix all the ingredients for the second marinade and dip the prawns in it. Thread the prawns on to the bamboo skewers, piercing the skewer through the tail of each prawn and taking it out through the tip of the head. Place on a baking tray and cook for 5–6 minutes in the preheated oven, then place under a hot grill for 1 minute and serve with the yoghurt rice and a salad of your choice.

PASTA MOILY

Everyone loves a Moily! Moily is a native Keralan coconut curry sauce that I have used here as a base for the pasta. This recipe is an excellent example of the fusion of East and West, where the spices and the sweetness of coconut blend perfectly with the pasta.

SERVES 4

200g dried or fresh pasta (such as fettuccini, spaghetti or penne)
2 tablespoons salt
2 tablespoons olive oil
2 teaspoons chopped coriander
grated Parmesan (if using vegetables or chicken, but omit if using seafood)

For the sauce
2 tablespoons vegetable oil
20 curry leaves
1 large onion, sliced
2.5cm piece of ginger, cut into matchsticks
4 hot green chillies, slit open lengthwise
½ teaspoon ground turmeric
200g seafood/vegetables/chicken (optional)
100ml chicken or fish stock (depending whether you are adding chicken or seafood) or water
200ml coconut milk
1 teaspoon salt

To make the sauce, heat the vegetable oil in a large frying pan. Add the curry leaves, onion, ginger and green chillies and stir for 15 minutes over a medium-low heat until the onions are soft. Add the turmeric, followed by the assorted vegetables, seafood or chicken, and stir for 30 seconds. Add the stock and coconut milk, cover and simmer for 5–6 minutes. If using seafood or chicken, simmer until they are cooked through.

Bring 1 litre of water and the salt to the boil in a large pot. Add the pasta and cook for about 10–12 minutes or as per instructions on the pack. If you have used a short pasta, it will take much less time. Stir occasionally until the pasta is cooked but still has a bite (al dente). Strain the pasta in a colander (and run under cold water if using at a later stage to stop further cooking) and pour over some olive oil. Toss to keep it separated.

Either toss the drained pasta into the sauce or adopt the classic way of plating by placing the hot pasta in a bowl and pouring the sauce on top. Sprinkle with chopped coriander and Parmesan, if using

PANEER AND PEAS CURRY

I almost completely forgot to include this important dish in the book, until I met with TV presenter Lisa Snowdon on the set of *Weekend Kitchen* and was able to squeeze it in just as my editor thought her work was done! This, I believe, is Lisa's favourite curry – she calls it 'cheesy peas'. It's yet to appear on any of the restaurant menus, but I've told Lisa that if she comes to Cinnamon Soho, we will cook it for her whenever she likes!

Known as *mutter paneer*, this is such a familiar dish in most Indian homes – everyone has their own tweaked version of it and mine is no different. If you wish, you can skip the stage of boiling tomatoes to make a purée, and use fresh tomato purée (you just need to cook the tomatoes longer before adding the cheese). In India we use paneer which is now available in most supermarkets in the UK too, but you can easily replace paneer with tofu, or halloumi cheese if you prefer.

SERVES 4

4 tomatoes
4 tablespoons vegetable oil
2 bay leaves
3 green cardamom pods
½ teaspoon cloves
1 teaspoon cumin seeds
2 large white onions, finely chopped
½ teaspoon ground turmeric
1 teaspoon ground coriander
1 teaspoon red chilli powder
1 teaspoon salt
2.5cm piece of ginger, finely chopped
2 green chillies, finely chopped
300g paneer, chopped into 1cm dice
200g frozen petit pois or green peas, thawed
1 teaspoon sugar
½ teaspoon garam masala
3 tablespoons single cream (optional)
2 tablespoons salted butter (optional)
freshly ground black pepper (optional)
2 tablespoons chopped coriander
juice of ½ lemon

Cut the tomatoes into quarters, then place in a deep pan with 200ml water. Cover with a lid and bring to the boil, then reduce to a simmer and cook for 20 minutes, until reduced to a purée.

Heat the oil in a frying pan, add the bay leaves, cardamom and cloves and let them sizzle and pop for a minute or so, then add the cumin seeds and as they crackle, stir to mix evenly. After 20–30 seconds, add the chopped onions and cook until golden brown, approximately 10–12 minutes with constant stirring to colour the onions evenly.

Add the turmeric, ground coriander, chilli powder and salt. Stir, mixing well, and cook for a minute or so. Then add the chopped ginger and chillies, sauté for a minute and add the cooked tomato purée. Reduce the heat, cover with a lid and cook the tomatoes down for 4–5 minutes until the onions and tomatoes come together. Now add the diced paneer (or tofu). Cook for 23 minutes mixing well, then add the petit pois.

Simmer for a minute, then sprinkle with the sugar and garam masala. Stir in the cream and butter, if using. Add a twist or two of cracked pepper from the mill, stir in chopped coriander and finish with squeeze of lemon.

Serve hot with parathas, poories or chapati, as you may choose.

DAY'S END

HABIJABI FRITTATA

This is my take on my wife Archana's quick fix of a lunch when we're short of either time or ingredients, or both. She adds onions, potatoes, spinach and mushrooms if we have any. However, I like to add meat in some form, so either a cooked sausage or cooking chorizo, plus roasted peppers, grilled aubergine… anything goes. Hence the name Habi-Jabi, which in Bengal means anything, everything, whatever.

SERVES 4-6

2 tablespoons olive oil
1 large or 2 medium starchy potatoes, peeled and sliced 3–4 mm thick
1 large onion, sliced
1 teaspoon cumin seeds
1 teaspoon chilli flakes
1 teaspoon sea salt
2 shiitake or portobello mushrooms, sliced 3–4mm thick
50g cooking chorizo or cooked tandoori chicken, sliced
a few slices of roasted red peppers (optional)
a few slices of grilled aubergine slices (optional)
a handful of spinach
6 eggs, beaten
2 spring onions, finely sliced
salt and freshly ground black pepper
1 tablespoon chopped coriander

Heat the oil in a medium non-stick frying pan over a medium heat. Add the potatoes and onion, fry for a minute, then add the cumin seeds, chilli flakes and salt. Continue cooking and stirring for 3–5 minutes until the onions begin to get some colour. Add the mushrooms and chorizo and cook for another 3–4 minutes until the vegetables begin to crisp up, then add the peppers, and aubergine, (or whatever you may be using), stir in the spinach and mix well over a high heat for a minute.

In a bowl, whisk together eggs, spring onions and some seasoning.

Tip the eggs into frying pan, mix quickly, lower the heat and cook for 5–7 minutes. Meanwhile, preheat the grill. Once the top side has almost set, pop under the grill for 1–2 minutes or until firm and golden.

Slide out of the pan. Sprinkle with green coriander and serve immediately with a salad of your choice.

WINTER VEGETABLE CURRY

This vegetable curry reminds me of winters in India and simple home cooking at its best. This humble vegetable curry is cooked in almost every household in northern India. Generally considered too mundane to put on restaurant menus, it is an all-time favourite at home, and comes in many guises – made with turnips instead of the vegetables listed below, for example, or served with lots of sauce to accompany rice. If the water is omitted, this semi-dry dish goes down a treat with poories (see page 14). I prefer the drier version, as the flavours are more pronounced.

SERVES 4

3 tablespoons vegetable or corn oil
1 bay leaf
4 green cardamom pods
1 teaspoon cumin seeds
3 onions, finely chopped
1 large potato, cut into 1 cm dice
2 carrots, cut into 1cm dice
3 ripe tomatoes, blended to a purée or very finely chopped
2.5cm piece of ginger, finely chopped
2 hot green chillies, cut in half lengthways
½ teaspoon ground turmeric
½ teaspoon red chilli powder
1 teaspoon ground cumin
1 teaspoon ground coriander
2 teaspoons salt
1 cauliflower, cut into 1cm florets

200g peas
juice of 1 lemon
2 tablespoons chopped coriander and/ or dill

Heat the oil in a heavy-based pan over a high heat. Add the bay leaf, cardamom pods and cumin seeds and let them crackle. Add the chopped onions and cook for 10 minutes over a fairly high heat, stirring occasionally, until light golden brown.

Add the potatoes and carrots and stir for a couple of minutes. Stir in the puréed tomatoes, ginger, green chillies, spices and salt and cook for 8–10 minutes, until the oil begins to separate from the mixture at the sides of the pan.

Add the cauliflower and cook, stirring, for 2 minutes, then add the peas and cook for 3 minutes. Pour in up to 450ml water, if you prefer a slightly wetter curry, and cook uncovered for about 10 minutes until the vegetables are tender but still retain a little bite.

Check the seasoning, then stir in the lemon juice and sprinkle with the chopped herbs. Serve hot with chapattis or deep-fried poories

INDIAN WINTER VEGETABLE PILAU

This is my mother's recipe for *subz mutter pulao*, a vegetable pilau usually reserved for important guests and special dinners, on New Year's Day she often makes this for us and orders a butter chicken from her local takeaway!

Traditionally in Lucknow and the central states, pilaus were very varied and made using several ingredients, often many used together. In fact, pilaus were considered to be more exotic and special, even more so than Biryanis which were often deemed to be 'rough and ready'.

SERVES 6-8

400g basmati rice
75g ghee
3 bay leaves
4 black cardamom pods
1 cinnamon stick
½ teaspoon cloves
1 teaspoon cumin seeds
2 red onions, finely sliced
1 carrot, cut into 1cm dice
100g cauliflower cut into 1cm florets
1 teaspoon ground turmeric
4 teaspoons salt
4 green chillies, slit lengthways
100g frozen petits pois or garden peas
2 tablespoons ready-to-eat raisins
1 teaspoon sugar (optional)
2 tablespoons chopped mint
2 tablespoons chopped coriander
50g cashew nuts, deep fried and
    coarsely chopped

Wash the rice in running water, then soak in cold water for 15–30 minutes as this reduces the cooking time and prevents the grains from breaking while cooking.

Heat the ghee in a large heavy-based pan, add all the whole spices except cumin seeds and allow them to crackle for a minute or so, then add the cumin seeds. As they begin to splutter, immediately add the sliced onions. Sauté for 3–5 minutes until they start changing colour.

Now add the carrot and cauliflower and stir to mix well, reduce the heat and sweat for 2–3 minutes. Add the turmeric, salt and green chillies and cook for another minute, stirring, until the turmeric is thoroughly mixed in.

Add the drained soaked rice. Mix lightly and carefully, stirring to mix all the ingredients together. Take care not to over-work the rice as the grains may break. After a minute or so, mix in the peas and raisins.

(At this stage, if you just wanted to get ahead but not finish the pilau just yet, you could remove the rice from the heat and allow to cool, then store in the fridge for a couple of days.)

When you're ready to finish the pilau, add 900ml boiling water to the sautéed rice and vegetable mix and bring to the boil again. Add the sugar, if using. Cook over a medium-high heat, stirring gently from time to time (but remember that too much handling can break the rice grains).

The water is nearly all absorbed when you can see small holes appearing on the surface of the rice. Sprinkle over the mint and the coriander, cover the pan with a tightly fitting lid and reduce the heat to a minimum for 8–10 minutes. Alternatively, place it in the oven at 125ºC/Gas Mark ¾ for 10 minutes for the rice to finish cooking. Sprinkle with fried cashew nuts and serve.

Alternatively, follow the recipe up to the stage of adding peas and raisins, pour 900ml cold water over the rice in the container and sprinkle with the mint and coriander. Cover with clingfilm, prick to make a few holes in the film and place in a microwave (800W) on high for 15 minutes. Allow the rice to rest for 5 minutes, then transfer to a serving dish. One of the wonders of modern technology!

BREAM WITH CHUTNEY AND CRISP RICE FLAKES

Crisp rice flakes were a staple snack in our home when I was growing up. Every evening in the winter when my dad returned from the office, my mother would make a snack of these fried crisp rice flakes, but each day the topping or the garnish would be slightly different. One day crispy onions and fried chilli, the next day seasoned peas, another day stir-fried cauliflower. I've used the same inspiration to serve a crisp piece of fish with tomato and coconut chutney.

SERVES 4

4 small fillets (120–150g each) of sea
    bream or sea bass
½ teaspoon salt
½ teaspoon onion seeds
1 teaspoon fennel seeds
½ teaspoon dried chilli flakes
    (optional)
a pinch of ground turmeric
1 tablespoon vegetable oil
juice of ½ lemon
4 tablespoons Tomato and Coconut
    Chutney (see page 191)

For the crisp rice
2 tablespoons vegetable oil
6 heaped tablespoons pressed rice
    flakes
1 tablespoon chopped coriander
½ teaspoon salt or Chaat Masala
    (see page 224)

Sprinkle the fish with the spices and seasoning and set aside for a few minutes. If the fillets are long, cut into two and serve two pieces in each portion.

To make the crisp rice, heat the oil in a small frying pan until smoking, then add the pressed rice flakes. They will begin to puff up, fry and curl almost immediately. Keep stirring to make sure they cook evenly. Cook for 2–3 minutes over a medium heat until all the rice flakes have been fried and crisped evenly. Add the coriander and salt, remove from the heat, tip on to a plate and allow to cool.

Wipe out the same pan, drizzle in the oil and cook the fish skin side down for 3–4 minutes over a medium heat until crisp, then turn over and cook for 2–3 minutes on the other side. Squeeze over the lemon and remove from the pan.

To serve, place the fillets in small, individual bowls and spoon over the chutney. Completely cover with the crisp rice flakes and serve immediately.

CURED SEA BREAM CEVICHE

Cured fish isn't a luxury commonly seen in Indian homes, but in line with how things change all the time, even home cooking changes. Originally inspired by a meal at Martin Morales' restaurant Ceviche, the introduction of a couple of spices and some diced mango are embellishments from the Singh household. We hope you enjoy!

SERVES 4-6

1 red onion, finely sliced
1 teaspoon fennel seeds
½ teaspoon nigella seeds
600g sea bream (or sea bass) fillets, skinned and boned
1 teaspoon salt, plus extra to season
juice of 8 limes
juice of 1 orange
1 red chilli, thinly sliced
50g coriander, roughly chopped
½ fresh mango, flesh chopped into 1cm dice
Mock Wasabi Chutney (see page 193)

Place the sliced onion in a bowl of iced water and soak for 5 minutes, then drain well.

Dry-roast the fennel and nigella seeds in a small pan for a couple of minutes until fragrant.

Cut the fish into 1.5–2cm cubes and rub with the salt. Place in a bowl and leave for 1 minute. Add the citrus juices, the roasted spices and the chilli, stir and leave to marinate for 10 minutes. Check the seasoning and adjust if necessary.

Scatter over the coriander, onion and mango and give it a mix. Divide the fish and marinade into four bowls and serve immediately with the Mock Wasabi chutney on the side.

CALCUTTA PUFFED RICE SALAD WITH CURED SALMON

I picked up this curing business from my very good friend, the inimitable Eric Chavot. We came up with this recipe which works beautifully as a starter dressed with lime, spices and mustard oil, and also as a great ingredient for an Indian-inspired salad or even a canapé served with spiced yoghurt on sliced cucumber! Here I love adding it to the quintessential Bengali street-food favourite, *jhaal muri* or puffed rice salad.

SERVES 6

For the cured salmon
675g salmon, boned
zest of 1 orange and 2 limes
120g coriander, leaves and stalks
    coarsely chopped
400g sea salt
400g sugar
4 teaspoons red chilli powder

For the topping
1 tablespoon finely chopped dill
½ teaspoon roasted cumin seeds

For the salad
1 teaspoon black onion seeds
1 large boiled potato, peeled and
    chopped into 1cm dice
1cm piece of ginger, finely chopped
1 green chilli, finely chopped
    (optional)
1 tablespoon chopped coriander
½ teaspoon sea salt
½ teaspoon sugar
juice of 1 lime
5 segments of lime, diced small
1–2 tablespoons mustard oil, to
    drizzle
100g puffed rice (available in most
    good Asian stores)
salad leaves, to garnish

Arrange the salmon fillets skin side down on a tray. Sprinkle with the citrus zest. Evenly spread with the chopped coriander and press lightly. Mix together the salt, sugar and chilli powder and spread some of the mixture onto another tray. Place the fillets on the mixture and then completely cover the top sides with the remaining mixture. Cover and leave to cure in the fridge for 8 hours or overnight. If necessary, weigh down the salmon to keep it immersed in the mixture.

After 8 hours, turn the fillets and leave for another 8 hours. Do this once again. After a total of 24 hours, remove the excess spice and salt from the fillets and wash the fillets. The fillets should feel quite firm on touch. Dry with kitchen paper.

Mix the two topping ingredients together and sprinkle evenly over the fillets. Cover and store in the fridge. The fish will keep for up to a week in the fridge.

To serve, cut the salmon into slices 5–8mm thick, then dice about 180g of the salmon and set aside.

Mix together all the other ingredients for salad, except the puffed rice, and leave for 5 minutes. When ready to serve, simply stir in the diced salmon and puffed rice and serve immediately alongside the sliced salmon and garnished with salad leaves of your choice.

BAKED COD WITH GREEN SPICES

This recipe states cod, but feel free to use any thick white fish, such as like pollack, haddock, coley or halibut. In my opinion, nigella and carom seeds partnered with any kind of fish is a match made in heaven. The sparing use of spices still allows for the flavours of the fish to be appreciated, and the Chickpea Curry (see page 181), with or without chorizo, makes for an excellent accompaniment. The green spiced breadcrumbs add colour, zing, and texture to the dish. Your guests will be impressed!

SERVES 4

4 x 180g fillets of cod
1 teaspoon nigella seeds
½ teaspoon carom seeds
1 teaspoon salt
1 tablespoon chopped coriander stalks
1cm piece of ginger, chopped
2 tablespoons vegetable oil
2 tablespoons butter
juice of 1 lemon

For the green spiced crumbs
100g Japanese panko breadcrumbs
3 tablespoons Green Coriander
  Chutney (see page 190)
½ teaspoon sugar

To make the spiced crumbs, Preheat oven to 80–90ºC/Gas Mark ½. Mix together the breadcrumbs, chutney and sugar. Spread the mixture out on a baking tray and dry in the warm oven for 30 minutes or so.

Preheat oven to 220ºC/Gas Mark 7.

Season the fish by sprinkling with the onion seeds, carom seeds, salt, coriander stalks and ginger, then set aside for 5 minutes to allow the seasoning to stick to the fish.

Heat a non-stick frying pan and drizzle with the oil. When the oil is hot, add the fish, skin side down, and cook over a high heat for 3–5 minutes (depending upon the thickness of the fish), without moving the fish. Let the skin get a nice crust, then add the butter and as it foams, spoon over the fish to cook in nut-brown butter. Turn the fish over and cook the other side for 3 minutes or so. Repeat the spooning of foaming butter on the other side too. Transfer the fish to an ovenproof dish, sprinkle generously with the spiced crumbs and bake in the preheated oven for just 3–4 minutes until the fish is cooked and the crust becomes crisp.

Remove the fish from the oven, squeeze with lemon juice and serve either on its own or with chickpea curry (see page 181) as an accompaniment.

CHILLED CRAB SALAD WITH TAMARIND

This is a chilled salad of crab with Keralan tamarind dressing. In this recipe, the delicacy and sweetness of crab meat is well married with tangy tamarind and pepper dressing. It is a perfect treat for crab lovers, and is very healthy too.

SERVES 4

1 head of cos or romaine lettuce or
   2 small baby gems
400g white crab meat
1cm piece of ginger, finely chopped
1 green chilli, finely chopped
1 tablespoon chopped coriander
¼ teaspoon salt

For the dressing
2 whole dried red chillies
2 shallots, thickly sliced
5 sprigs of curry leaves
1 teaspoon black peppercorns,
   crushed
4 tablespoons tamarind pulp
   (available in cans)
1 tablespoon vegetable oil
salt
sugar, to taste

To make the dressing, toast the red chillies in a pan or a hot oven until they are almost burnt. Mix with the shallots, curry leaves and peppercorns and grind them coarsely using a pestle and mortar or a blender. Mix the tamarind pulp with the ground spices and oil. Season to taste with the salt and sugar and refrigerate.

Cut the lettuce head into quarters, then wash well in cold water to remove any grit or earth. Dip the lettuce in a bowl of iced water for a minute or so until the leaves crisp up. Drain on kitchen paper, then dress with crab meat, ginger, chilli, salt and coriander and drizzle with the dressing. Serve immediately.

CRAB AND CURRY LEAF RISOTTO

We all love good risotto, and this one with crab and curry leaf packs a good punch. You can also substitute the crab with shrimps or small prawns if you prefer.

SERVES 4-6

500ml hot chicken or fish stock
2 tablespoons olive oil
20–30 curry leaves
2 small onions, finely chopped
400g risotto rice
2 garlic cloves, crushed
4cm piece of ginger, chopped
3 tablespoons white wine vinegar
   (optional)
250g white crab meat, picked
1 fresh red chilli, finely chopped
zest and juice of 3 limes

In a large saucepan, bring the stock and an additional 600ml water to the boil.

Meanwhile, heat the olive oil in a large, deep, lidded non-stick frying pan. Fry 15–20 curry leaves for 2–3 minutes until crisp, then remove from the oil, drain and set aside.

Add the onions to the same pan, reduce the heat to low and cook with the lid on for 3–4 minutes until soft, stirring occasionally. Add the rice, remaining curry leaves, crushed garlic and ginger and stir for 1–2 minutes until fragrant. Then add the vinegar, if using, and reduce for a couple of minutes.

Add half the hot liquid (stock and water) to the pan of rice and simmer for 8–10 minutes, stirring occasionally.

If using fresh crab, scoop out all the crab meat from the shell, reserving the nicest pieces to garnish, and stir the rest into the pan with the remaining stock. Cook for a further 6–8 minutes, adding the remaining stock as needed, until the rice is tender.

Stir in the chilli, lime juice and half the zest. Season to taste. Divide between four bowls and scatter with the crisp fried curry leaves, reserved crab and lime zest, then serve immediately.

PRAWN BIRYANI

Unlike my other biryani recipes, this one is really quick (apart from half an hour of marinating) and simple. Prawns are quick to cook and the fresh herbs and spices make for a refreshingly light, simple and quick biryani still packed with flavour.

SERVES 4

400g small shelled raw prawns
250g basmati rice
vegetable oil, for deep frying
2 large onions, sliced
50g ghee
1 teaspoon black peppercorns
3 cloves
2 green cardamom pods
1 star anise
10 curry leaves
1 tablespoon dry shrimp paste
4 green chillies, slit
2 tablespoons chopped mint
2 tablespoons chopped coriander
½ teaspoon ground turmeric
1½ teaspoons salt
500ml fish stock or water

For the marinade
2 tablespoons vegetable oil
1 tablespoon red chilli powder
1½ teaspoons garam masala
1½ teaspoons salt
20 curry leaves, finely chopped
1 teaspoon sugar
zest and juice of 1 lime

Mix all the marinade ingredients together, add the prawns and set aside for 30 minutes.

Wash the rice in running water. Soak in cold water for 15 minutes, then drain.

Heat the oil in the deep fat fryer to 180ºC, add the onions and fry for 5–6 minutes or until golden. Remove and drain.

Heat the ghee in a wide heavy-based pan over a high heat. Add the whole spices and when they crackle, add the fried onions. Reduce the heat to medium, add the shrimp paste and green chillies and sauté for 1 minute.

Add the mint, coriander, turmeric, salt, rice and the fish stock or water and bring to the boil. When most of the liquid has been absorbed, you will see small holes on the surface of rice in the casserole – at this stage, lower the heat and scatter over the marinated prawns. Cover with a tight fitting lid and cook for 4–5 minutes (the prawns will cook in the steam).

Remove the lid and stir to mix the prawns through the rice, remove from heat, then put the lid back and set aside for 5 minutes for the flavours to mix through, and the biryani to rest.

Allow to cool slightly, then serve with curried yoghurt (see page 225) and green coconut chutney (page 190).

KING PRAWNS IN COCONUT CURRY SAUCE

hingri malai curry is one of the all-time favourite Bengali dishes, reserved for very special guests, big celebratory dinners, weddings and so on. I remember this dish once served inside a green tender coconut. As a child, I was told the term *malai* refers to the creamy flesh inside the green coconut that can be enjoyed while tucking into the coconut. It made sense then and it makes sense now as this is how most people relate to the dish. While travelling and working as a chef, it surprised me no end to see the similarity between this dish and a Malaysian laksa, and I wonder if the Bengali name originated from 'Malaya', as it is known in India.

The period between Dussehra (Durga Puja in Bengal) and Diwali (Kali Puja in Bengal) is a period described as Bijoya or victory. During Bijoya, people visit family, friends and their entire social circle, taking sweets, exchanging gifts and eating together. Forgetting to visit someone over Bijoya is the Bengali equivalent of dropping someone from your Christmas card list! One of my earliest food memories is eating this delicious prawn curry at a Bijoya dinner.

SERVES 2

400g freshwater prawns (the largest size you can find), peeled and deveined (peeled weight)
1 teaspoon ground turmeric
1 teaspoon salt
3 tablespoons vegetable oil
2 bay leaves
3 red onions (around 275g), blended to a fine paste
1 tablespoon ground cumin
2 tablespoons Ginger and Garlic Paste (see page 226)
2 green chillies, slit lengthways
250ml shellfish stock
75ml coconut milk
½ teaspoon sugar (optional)
4–5 green cardamom pods, ground
1 tablespoon chopped coriander
juice of ½ lime

Marinate the prawns with half the turmeric and half the salt for 5 minutes.

Heat half the oil in a pan and add the bay leaves and onion paste and sauté over a medium heat for 10–12 minutes until very light brown.

Meanwhile, heat the remaining oil in a non-stick frying pan and sear the prawns briefly for 1–2 minutes, turning them to sear on each side, then set aside.

Mix the remaining turmeric, the ground cumin and ginger-garlic paste in 75ml water. Add to the sautéed onions, reduce the heat and cook for 2–3 minutes, stirring regularly. Add the remaining salt, green chillies and prawns and stir for 1 minute. Add the stock, then mix in the coconut milk and simmer for 2–3 minutes or just until the prawns are cooked, adding a little more stock if necessary. Correct the seasoning with salt and sugar and sprinkle on the ground cardamom and chopped coriander. Squeeze over the lime juice and serve with rice.

This is best eaten with fresh boiled basmati rice, enriched with a tablespoon of ghee or cold salted butter, a pinch of smoked sea salt and freshly cracked pepper. Add the butter, salt and pepper to hot steaming rice, mix and serve immediately.

MULLET IN A BENGALI PRAWN AND VEGETABLE BROTH

The Bengalis are often noted as being *buddhiman manush* or intelligent people, and this is often ascribed to the fact that they eat a lot of fish. This recipe is my take on the classic Bengali dish *macher johl*. Having grown up in Asansol, I would normally use a fish like rohu or katla with the bone, but here I recommend a flat fish like mullet which can be filleted. The fillet is served on the broth made of potatoes, aubergine, and tomato, rather than in it – this allows a better appreciation of the textures and also makes eating it easier. In its traditional form, this is a typical homely dish that is flexible, forgiving and easily extended. A little bit of fish can go a long way!

SERVES 4

4 small fillets of red mullet, scaled and pin boned
4 scallops (optional)
80g prawns or squid (optional)
1 teaspoon salt
¼ teaspoon ground turmeric
1 teaspoon red chilli powder
3 tablespoons mustard or vegetable oil

For the sauce
2 tablespoons mustard oil
4 green cardamom pods, crushed
6 peppercorns
2 bay leaves
½ teaspoon black onion seeds
½ teaspoon fennel seeds
2 onions, finely chopped
¼ teaspoon ground turmeric
1 teaspoon red chilli powder
1½ teaspoons ground cumin, roasted
2 small aubergines, cut into quarters
2 small potatoes, cut into quarters
50g small prawns, peeled and deveined (optional)
500ml fish stock or hot water
1¼ teaspoons salt
2 tomatoes, cut into quarters
½ teaspoon sugar
2 green chillies, slit lengthways
2 tablespoons chopped coriander

To make the sauce, heat the mustard oil in a pan over a high heat. When the oil is hot, add the cardamom, peppercorns, bay leaves, onion seeds and fennel seeds and let them crackle. Add the onions and cook for 6–8 minutes until golden brown. Add the turmeric, chilli powder and cumin and sauté for a minute. Add the aubergines, potatoes and prawns and sauté for 3 minutes. Now add the fish stock or hot water and salt and simmer for 15 minutes.

Meanwhile, wash the fish and pat dry with kitchen paper. Sprinkle the fillets and seafood with salt, turmeric and chilli powder. Heat the oil in a pan and fry the fillets over a high heat for 2–3 minutes until browned and caramelised on the under side, then turn and cook on the other side for 2–3 minutes.

When the sauce looks like a thin broth, add the cooked fish and tomatoes and simmer for 3 minutes. Add the sugar, green chillies, coriander and fried fish/seafood to the sauce and simmer for a couple of minutes, allowing the flavours to mix together.

Place the sauce in a deep bowl with the fillets and seafood on top in a criss-cross fashion and serve immediately with steamed rice.

Tip: If you are not too fond of the strong flavour of mustard oil, then heat it over a high heat; when it smokes, allow it to cool down. Reheat the oil and the pungent raw flavour of the mustard will have disappeared.

CHICKEN 65

This is what most of south India ate in the 1980s until we discovered the joys of Indo-Chinese chilli chicken. There are many myths about how the dish got its name 65: some say it was the 65th dish on the menu, some claim it took 65 goes to perfect the recipe, while others say it was a regular guest in Room 65 of the hotel who always ordered his dish this way... All we know is that it tastes delicious both as a starter and as a snack with drinks.

SERVES 2

2 skinless chicken (or duck) breasts, around 400g, diced into 2.5cm cubes
vegetable oil, for deep frying
finely chopped fresh coriander, ginger and green chillies, to garnish (optional)

For the first marinade
2.5cm piece of ginger, chopped
2 garlic cloves, chopped
3 teaspoons red chilli powder
1 teaspoon salt
2 tablespoons yoghurt

For the second marinade
1 tablespoon Ginger and Garlic Paste (see page 226)
1 egg
2 tablespoons cornflour
½ teaspoon sugar
juice of ½ lemon

For the tempering
3 tablespoons vegetable oil
10 curry leaves
3 garlic cloves, chopped
2.5cm piece of ginger, chopped
1 green chilli, finely chopped
½ teaspoon salt
1 pinch of sugar
50g spring onions or red onion, chopped (optional)
2 tablespoons full-fat yoghurt
juice of ½ lemon

Mix all the ingredients for the first marinade in a bowl. Add the chicken and leave to marinate for 10–20 minutes.

Mix together the ingredients for second marinade in another bowl. Remove the chicken pieces from the first marinade and dip in the second one.

Heat the oil in a deep-fat fryer to 160–170ºC. Deep-fry the chicken for 3–5 minutes until golden and crispy. Drain on kitchen paper and keep warm.

For the tempering, heat the oil in a wok, add the curry leaves, ginger, garlic and green chillies and sauté over a high heat for 1 minute.

Add the chicken to the wok and toss it until it is coated with the mixture in the wok. Add the salt, sugar and spring onions and cook over a high heat while stirring for another 1–2 minutes, until the sugar begins to caramelise but not burn. Keep the heat up high and stir in the yoghurt little by little, stirring continuously to prevent the yoghurt splitting. Finish with a squeeze of lemon, check the seasoning, garnish and serve immediately.

CHICKEN WINGS WITH CRACKED BLACK PEPPER

These chicken wings aren't anything like the deep-fried 'buffalo wings' we come across in fast-food restaurants. Rather, this is a Kerala toddy shop number that works just as well with bread as a main course as it does with a few drinks as a canapé or nibbles. It's the peppercorn which is the real hero as far as the spice is concerned and it's easy to see how it may help down the arrack in the toddy shop!

SERVES 4

600g chicken wings
oil, for deep-frying

For the marinade
1 teaspoon Ginger and Garlic Paste (see page 226)
1½ teaspoons salt
1½ teaspoons red chilli powder
juice of ½ lemon
½ teaspoon black peppercorns, coarsely crushed
60g cornflour

For the stir-fry sauce
2 tablespoons vegetable or corn oil
1 green cardamom pod
2.5cm piece of cinnamon stick
1 large onion, finely chopped
1 teaspoon salt
1 teaspoon red chilli powder
1 teaspoon black peppercorns, coarsely crushed
2 tomatoes, finely chopped

1 tablespoon chopped coriander
2.5cm piece of ginger, finely chopped
1 green chilli, finely chopped
juice of ½ lemon, or to taste
a pinch of sugar, to taste

Mix together all the ingredients for the marinade and rub them over the chicken wings. Set aside to marinate for 15 minutes.

In the meantime, make the sauce for the stir fry. Heat the oil in a pan; add the cardamom and cinnamon, onion and salt. Cook over a low-medium heat for 5–6 minutes. Add the chilli powder, crushed peppercorns and tomatoes, stirring continuously. Simmer over a low-medium heat for 3–5 minutes until the liquid has evaporated. Finish the sauce with chopped fresh coriander, chopped ginger and chillies and lemon juice. Taste the sauce – you may need to add a pinch of sugar.

Heat the oil in a deep fat fryer to 180°C. Add the chicken pieces and fry for 6–8 minutes, until cooked and crisp on the outside. Alternatively, preheat oven to 220°C/Gas Mark 7 and cook drizzled in a little oil on a baking tray for 35 minutes, turning halfway through the cooking time. Drain the chicken on kitchen paper.

Add the cooked chicken to the pan of sauce and stir fry over a high heat for a couple of minutes until the chicken pieces are nicely wrapped in the sauce. Check the seasoning and serve immediately.

OLD DELHI-STYLE BUTTER CHICKEN

Butter chicken has to be India's favourite dish when eating out. I must have asked hundreds of people to name the one dish they always order when they go out and Butter Chicken has featured in every response! As for me personally, this is the best dish ever – it has sugar and spice, kick and texture, creamy unctiousness and bite, all at the same time.

SERVES 4

2 x 750g free-range young chickens (poussin), skinned and cut in half along the backbone (alternatively, use 800g boned chicken thighs, cut into two)

For the marinade
80g full-fat Greek yoghurt
1 tablespoon Ginger and Garlic Paste (see page 226)
1 tablespoon vegetable oil
1½ teaspoons salt
juice of 1 lemon
1 tablespoon red chilli powder
1 teaspoon ground cumin
½ teaspoon garam masala

For the sauce
1kg tomatoes, halved
5cm piece of ginger, half crushed and half finely chopped
4 garlic cloves, peeled
4 green cardamom pods
5 cloves

1 bay leaf
1 tablespoon red chilli powder
80g butter, diced
2 green chillies, slit lengthways
75ml single cream
1 teaspoon salt
1 tablespoon dried fenugreek leaves, crushed between your fingertips
½ teaspoon garam masala
1 tablespoon sugar

First, prepare the chicken. Make small cuts all over the chicken pieces with a sharp knife to help the marinade penetrate. To prepare the marinade, mix all the ingredients together in a deep ovenproof dish. Smear the cut chicken with the marinade, cover and set aside in the fridge for 10 minutes.

Preheat oven to 220ºC/Gas Mark 7.

Cook the chicken in the preheated oven for 13–15 minutes. You may need to turn the pieces after 8–10 minutes or so to ensure they colour evenly on both sides. The chicken does not need to be completely cooked at this point as it will continue to cook in the sauce. Cut the chicken halves into smaller pieces. Strain off the juices through a fine sieve and set aside.

For the sauce, place the tomatoes in a pan with 125ml water, the crushed ginger, garlic, cardamom, cloves and bay leaf and simmer for

about 10 minutes over medium heat until the tomatoes have completely disintegrated. Pick out the larger spices, then blend the tomato broth with a hand-held blender and pass it through a sieve to obtain a smooth purée. Return the purée to a clean pan, add the chilli powder and simmer for 12–15 minutes. It should slowly begin to thicken.

When the sauce turns glossy, add the chicken pieces and the reserved roasting juices. Then add 200–250ml water and simmer for 3–5 minutes until the sauce turns glossy again and the water is absorbed (for a thicker sauce, either add slightly less water or simmer for a little longer).

Slowly whisk in the butter, a couple of pieces at a time, and simmer for 6–8 minutes, until the chicken is cooked through and the sauce is beginning to acquire a glaze. Add the chopped ginger, green chillies and cream and simmer for a minute or two longer, taking care that the sauce does not split. Stir in the salt, crushed fenugreek leaves and garam masala, then check the seasoning and add the sugar. Serve with naan bread (see page 169) or pilau rice.

Eat what you can, then store any leftover chicken and sauce in the fridge. Leftovers make a great filling for ravioli (see page 154–155).

103

DAY'S END

CHARGRILLED GUINEA FOWL WITH PEANUT SAUCE

This is a really simple starter which draws its inspiration from Thai cooking. As a variation of this dish, wrap the pieces of guinea fowl breast in pandan leaves and then grill them. You can also thin down the sauce and serve a larger portion with rice as an interesting main course.

SERVES 4

4 guinea fowl breast, skin removed
   and cut into 2.5cm dice
12 bamboo skewers

For the marinade
1 lemongrass stick
1 teaspoon red chilli powder
1 tablespoon Ginger and Garlic Paste
   (see page 226)
1 teaspoon salt
½ teaspoon sugar
2 fresh lime leaves, cut into fine strips
juice of 1 lime
1 tablespoon vegetable oil

For the sauce
125ml peanut or vegetable oil
100g raw peanuts, skinned
2–3 fresh Thai red chillies
1cm piece of ginger, sliced
4 garlic cloves
125ml coconut milk
1 tablespoon fish sauce
2 teaspoons dark soy sauce
1 tablespoon sugar
juice of 1 lemon
pinch of salt
2 tablespoons chopped coriander

Soak the bamboo skewers in water for 30 minutes.

Meanwhile, for the marinade, make the lemongrass stalk into a paste by removing the outer leaves, chopping the stalk and then blending to a paste. Mix with all the marinade ingredients in a large bowl. Add the cubed guinea fowl breast and set aside to marinate for 15 minutes.

To make the sauce, heat the oil in a saucepan until it is almost smoking. Turn off the heat. Cool the oil a little and add the peanuts. The peanuts should cook to a golden brown in 2–3 minutes. You may have to turn on the heat again, but stir the peanuts constantly if you do, otherwise they may burn.

Using a slotted spoon, transfer the peanuts to a food processor or blender, along with the peanut oil and blend to a rough paste. Add the chillies, ginger and garlic, and continue to blend. Add the remaining sauce ingredients apart from the coriander and lemon juice and blend to a smooth paste. Stir in the coriander and set aside.

Preheat the grill to high.

Thread the guinea fowl onto the skewers and cook under the grill for 5–6 minutes or until cooked through, turning the skewers occasionally. Remove and squeeze the lemon juice over. Serve hot, with the peanut sauce at room temperature.

VENISON KOFTA

In my restaurants I love using game when in season and I particularly like its rich, bold flavours. However, at home I don't use any of the elaborate recipes using expensive cuts. This meatball version with spices and prunes for added depth of flavour is a simple dish to make either as a light lunch or to cook on a barbecue, or to serve with black lentils for a great dinner option.

SERVES 6-8

1kg venison, boneless and cut into chunks
250g suet
250g prunes, chopped
250g Jerusalem artichoke, peeled, cut into small chunks, then boiled until soft and cooked through
50g piece of ginger, peeled
5–6 garlic cloves, peeled
50g fresh coriander stalks and leaves
1½ tablespoons red chilli powder
1 teaspoon garam masala
20g salt
50ml vegetable oil
3 red onions, finely chopped

Mix the venison in a bowl with all the other ingredients except the onions and oil and leave aside for 30 minutes. Heat half the oil in a pan and sauté the onions until they are soft. Remove from the heat and allow to cool. Mince the venison mixture once in the food processor, then add the onions and mix well. Shape into patties weighing around 60g (more or less golf-ball sized).

Heat the remaining oil in a pan over a medium heat and cook the kofta for 2–3 minutes on each side until they are cooked but still moist inside. Serve on a bed of black lentils.

GRILLED VENISON ESCALOPES

These Rajasthan-style escalopes of venison may look complicated but they are pretty simple to make and quick to cook, and the results are equally impressive on a barbecue, too.

SERVES 4

600g leg or haunch of venison, deboned, fat trimmed and sliced into escalopes 3–4 mm thick
lemon juice, to serve

For the first marinade
2 teaspoons salt
1½ teaspoons red chilli powder
1 tablespoon Ginger and Garlic Paste (see page 226)
2 tablespoons pineapple juice
juice of 1 lemon

For the spice mix
4 green cardamom pods
½ teaspoon peppercorns
½ teaspoon cloves
1 tablespoon coriander seeds
1 tablespoon fennel seeds
1 tablespoon stone flower moss (optional, see page 231)

For the second marinade
2 tablespoons yoghurt
1 teaspoon sugar
2 tablespoons coriander stalks, finely chopped
2 tablespoons Crisp Fried Onions (see page 224)
2 tablespoons mustard or vegetable oil

For the mint lassi
200g yoghurt
100ml water
½ teaspoon cumin seeds, roasted and crushed
1 tablespoon chopped mint
1 teaspoon salt
1 teaspoon sugar

Mix together the lassi ingredients to make a thin smoothie-style drink. Chill in the fridge until the escalopes are cooked, then serve in glasses.

Mix the salt, chilli, ginger-garlic paste, pineapple juice and the lemon juice together in a bowl, then add the escalopes and set aside for 15 minutes.

Heat a small frying pan and dry-roast the cardamom, peppercorns, cloves, coriander seeds, fennel seeds and lichen, if using, for 3–4 minutes, stirring constantly to roast evenly. Let cool and grind coarsely. Smear the spice mix on to the escalopes.

Mix together the yoghurt, sugar, coriander and crisp onions into the escalopes and set aside for another 5–10 minutes to marinate and for the flavours to develop.

Cook the escalopes for a couple of minutes on each side on a hot grill pan or on a barbecue until medium-rare and serve with lemon juice squeezed over. Serve with glasses of mint lassi on the side.

As a variation, serve sprinkled with chopped vegetables like carrots, cucumber, coriander chutney etc as a garnish.

SOUTH INDIAN-STYLE STIR-FRIED SIRLOIN STEAK

This recipe is inspired by a traditional Kerala toddy shop favourite, *Beef Chukka* – a double-cooked beef dish where strips from chuck of beef, topside or skirt are first braised, then stir-fried with onions, curry leaves and more spices to make an excellent accompaniment to drinks. Here I have replaced the tough gristly beef with beautiful sirloin steak. It would be a shame to double-cook sirloin, so the steak is first grilled, then lightly stir-fried with the spices.

SERVES 2-4

3 tablespoons vegetable or corn oil
500g sirloin steak
5cm piece of ginger, cut into thin strips
4 garlic cloves, chopped
2 green chillies, halved lengthwise
12 curry leaves
3 red onions, cut into slices 5mm thick
1 teaspoon salt
3 tablespoons coconut milk
1 tablespoon chopped coriander
juice of ½ lime

For the spice mix
2 whole dried red chillies
1 tablespoon coriander seeds
½ teaspoon ground turmeric
1 tablespoon fennel seeds
1 teaspoon cumin seeds
½ teaspoon black peppercorns
5cm piece of cinnamon stick
3 cloves
2 green cardamom pods

To make the spice mix, dry roast all the spices in a pan, then crush them coarsely using a pestle and mortar. Sprinkle 2 pinches of the coarse spice mix on each side of the steak and set aside for 5 minutes.

Heat 1 tablespoon of the oil to smoking point in a frying pan, or a grill pan, and sear the steak over a high heat on one side for 2–3 minutes without moving it in the pan. Turn over on to the second side and cook another 3 minutes. Remove the steak from the heat and set aside to rest for 5 minutes.

While the meat is resting, heat the remaining oil in a second frying pan and add the ginger, garlic, green chillies, curry leaves and onions. Sauté for a couple of minutes until the onions have softened. Sprinkle in the salt and the remaining ground spice mix and stir-fry for another 2 minutes. Reduce the heat to medium, stir in the coconut milk and continue cooking until the liquid evaporates.

Slice the seared steak into strips 1cm wide and toss in the pan. Sprinkle in the coriander leaves, squeeze over the lime juice and serve immediately with naan bread (see page 169), paratha (see page 171) or steamed rice.

LAMB ROGAN JOSH

112

This could be made with whole shanks, but it's better made with shanks cut into three or four pieces (which are easier to fit into the pan and take less cooking time), like you would for an osso bucco. This dish would be just as good made with mutton or goat.

Not a lot of people know this, but 'rogan josh' literally translated from Hindi means 'red juice'. It's a Kashmiri dish where the redness comes from the bark of a locally grown tree called rattan jyoth. It is more than likely that you will not be able to find this even in Asian shops, so I suggest you use crushed beetroot in the final tempering process instead.

SERVES 4

6 lamb shanks, each shank cut into three or four pieces on the bone (ask your butcher to do this for you)
5 tablespoons corn oil or ghee
2 black cardamom pods, lightly crushed using a pestle and mortar
2 cinnamon sticks
½ teaspoon black peppercorns
2 large onions, finely chopped
1½ teaspoons salt
2 tablespoons Ginger and Garlic Paste (see page 226)
1½ tablespoons Kashmiri chilli powder
½ teaspoon ground coriander seeds
200ml plain yoghurt
400ml lamb stock or water
1 teaspoon ground ginger
1 teaspoon ground fennel seeds
½ teaspoon garam masala
2 tablespoons cream
1 tablespoon chopped coriander

Tempering (optional)
1 tablespoon ghee
2 sticks of rattan jyoth (see introduction) or half a crushed beetroot, to add colour

Pat the cut lamb shanks dry with kitchen paper and keep aside.

Heat the oil or ghee in a heavy-based casserole dish that you have a lid for, add the crushed cardamom, cinnamon sticks and peppercorns and stir over a high heat for 30 seconds or so until they release their flavours into the oil. Add the cut shanks and salt, sear over a high heat for about 10 minutes, turning frequently to brown the meat on all sides. Take care not to overload the pan as this would simply leach the juices out and stew the meat. Once browned, remove the meat and drain on kitchen paper.

Into the same pan, add the onions and salt, cook over a medium heat for 15 minutes or until golden brown. Add the ginger and garlic paste and cook for a couple of minutes. The paste tends to stick to the pan, so keep stirring continuously.

Now add the fried lamb, chilli powder and ground coriander and cook for a further 2–3 minutes. Take care to handle the shanks carefully so the meat does not come off the bone at this stage. Whisk in the yoghurt gradually, stirring continuously until it gets absorbed into the mix. Once all the yoghurt is absorbed, add the stock or water. Take care not to add all the yoghurt at once as it will lower the temperature of the sauce and the yoghurt will split.

Cover with a tight lid and cook over a low heat for 50–60 minutes until the shanks are soft (or around 2 hours if using whole shanks). You may need to add some more stock or water if the sauce is thick or it requires more moisture to cook. If you do not have a suitable pan, the pot-roasted and browned meat could be put in a braising tray with the liquid, covered with foil and braised in the oven (160–170ºC/Gas Mark 3–3½) for about 2 hours. (Although it's not traditional to finish this dish off in the oven, I find the results are much better if the last part of the cooking happens in an oven, as the textures are much better and the meat does not get broken.)

Check that the meat is cooked; it should easily fall off the bone when it's done. Sprinkle in the ground ginger, fennel and garam masala.

For a special finishing touch, tie up the rattan jyoth/beetroot in a muslin cloth. Heat the ghee in a pan, add the rattan jyoth/beetroot and let it infuse for a minute. Add the infused ghee to the shanks and simmer for 2 minutes. When the sauce turns dark red in colour, take out and discard the muslin.

Remove the meat from the sauce to a serving plate. Add the cream and chopped coriander to the pan and bring the sauce back to a simmer, then pour over the meat.

Serve with either steamed/ boiled basmati rice or a bread of your choice. Use any leftover rogan josh as a filling in the Lamb Rogan Josh Pithivier – the perfect party pie (see page 114).

LAMB ROGAN JOSH PITHIVIER

This pie is inspired by the British love for a good Rogan Josh. I find it very difficult to throw away small quantities of leftover food, so this dish provides a way to turn them into something small but beautifully formed. Alternatively, most combinations of root vegetables can be used here to extend the meat.

SERVES 6

500g all-butter puff pastry plain flour,for rolling out the pastry
400g leftover Lamb Rogan Josh curry (see pages 112–113), bone removed and meat chopped into 1cm dice
200g cooked Jerusalem artichokes, or roasted carrots, beetroot, parsnips (any root veg really)
100ml sauce or masala from the curry
1 red onion, finely chopped
1 green chilli, finely chopped
1 teaspoon finely chopped coriander
juice of 1 lemon
1 egg, beaten
melted butter, for drizzling

For the raita
1 cucumber, peeled, seeded and cut into 5mm dice
½ teaspoon salt
1 teaspoon sugar
1 teaspoon cumin seeds, roasted and crushed
100ml thick Greek yoghurt

Roll out the pastry on a well-floured surface until it is 2–3mm thick. Cut it into two circles, one 28cm in diameter and the other 25cm. Place both circles, separated by baking parchment, on a lined baking tray and rest in the fridge for 30 minutes.

To make the pie filling, mix the diced cooked lamb with the other vegetables, sauce, onion, chilli, coriander, lemon juice and seasoning.

Put the smaller pastry circle on a parchment-lined baking tray. Brush a 2cm border of egg all around and spread the meat filling on top. Drizzle with butter, then lay the larger pastry circle on top, letting the sides hang down to meet the border of the bottom circle. Seal the edge well, and use the back of a fork to create a neat pattern along the edge.

Brush the pithivier with beaten egg. With a small knife, cut a small cross in the top for steam to escape, then use the blunt edge of the knife to make a pattern of parallel semi-circles starting from near the cross and ending at the edge. Rest in the fridge for 30 minutes.

Meanwhile, make the raita. Place the cucumber dice in a bowl, stir in the salt and set aside for 15 minutes. Tip the cucumber into a piece of muslin, gather up the ends of the cloth and squeeze to drain off excess liquid. Put the cucumber back in the bowl and fold in the sugar, cumin and yoghurt. Set aside for 10–15 minutes to chill while you bake the pie.

Preheat oven to 200ºC/Gas Mark 6.

Place the pithivier in the oven and bake for 15–18 minutes, then reduce the temperature to 180ºC/Gas Mark 4 and bake for a further 10 minutes. Check that the pastry base is cooked before removing from the oven (cook for a few more minutes if necessary). Leave to rest for 20 minutes and serve warm with the cucumber raita.

AGRA AKHNI PULAO

The all-pervading Mughal influence on northern India can be easily seen in this recipe. Strategically placed on the spice route, Agra developed an excellent spice market which served most of Uttar Pradesh, Kashmir and Punjab too. The city gets its name from aagar, which means station, as it was a busy town with merchants coming in and out.

SERVES 4

For the yakhni (stock)
12 lamb chops
3 green cardamom pods
2 black cardamom pods
2 bay leaves
2.5cm piece of cinnamon stick
5 cloves
1 teaspoon black peppercorns
1cm piece of fresh ginger, crushed
3 garlic cloves, crushed
2 tablespoons corn oil
1 onion, sliced
1 litre lamb stock or water
1 tablespoon salt
100ml natural yoghurt, whisked
100ml milk

For the pulao
200g basmati rice
2 tablespoons ghee, plus an extra tablespoon for spooning over at the end
2 bay leaves
3 green cardamom pods

½ teaspoon mace
1 onion, sliced
½ teaspoon garam masala
few drops of rosewater (optional)
few drops of screwpine essence (optional; sold as kewra water in most good Asian stores and online)
seeds of ½ pomegranate

To make the yakhni, wash the lamb chops well in cold water. Tie all the whole spices, ginger and garlic in a piece of muslin to make a bouquet garni.

Heat the corn oil in a large pan and cook the onions for about 10 minutes over a medium heat until translucent, then move the onions to one side of the pan and add the lamb chops and sear them for 2–3 minutes until beginning to brown. Cover with the stock or water, add the bouquet garni and salt and simmer, uncovered, for 15 minutes over a low heat.

Whisk in the yoghurt and milk and simmer further for 10 minutes. Remove the lamb chops from the stock and keep aside. Strain the stock, squeezing the bouquet garni to extract maximum flavour. (Make sure you have at least 500ml stock, if less, top it up by adding more stock or water.)

To make the pulao, wash the rice in running water three or four times, then soak in warm water for 15 minutes, then drain.

Heat the ghee in a heavy-based pan and add the whole spices. When they start to crackle, add the onion and fry until golden. Reserve some of the onion slices for the garnish.

Add the drained rice to the pan and stir slowly over a low heat for 2–3 minutes to coat the rice with oil, onions and spices but not break the grains, then add the cooked lamb chops. Add the strained stock and bring to a boil, then reduce to a simmer.

When the stock is almost absorbed (approximately 8 minutes), sprinkle over the garam masala and spoon a tablespoon of ghee over the rice, then sprinkle with rosewater or screwpine essence, if using. Reduce the heat, cover the pan with a tight lid and cook for another 5 minutes (alternatively, finish it in an oven at 180ºC/Gas Mark 4 for 8–10 minutes).

Rest the pulao off the heat for another 5 minutes, garnish with the reserved fried onions and fresh pomegranate seeds strewn like jewels!

ENTERTAINING

POPCORN

This is my favourite movie snack of all time. We can never agree whether we prefer the sweet or savoury ones more, so we often make both!

SERVES 6-8

100g bag of sweet popping corn
100g bag of salted popping corn
50g butter
½ teaspoon ground turmeric
½ teaspoon salt
1 teaspoon sugar
2 tablespoons chopped coriander
½ teaspoon Chaat Masala (see page 224)

For the sweet popcorn
200g sugar

Pop the bags of popcorn in the microwave and cook as per the packet instructions. When the corn stops popping it is ready to take out of the microwave.

Melt the butter in a pan over a low heat with the turmeric, salt, sugar, chopped coriander and chaat masala. Add the popped corn to the pan and mix it through so it turns yellow with the spice coating evenly distributed. Remove from the heat, tip the popcorn out on to a large tray and allow to cool.

Divide the salted popcorn into two bowls and set one aside.

To make the sweet popcorn, place the sugar in a large deep frying pan with 100ml water. Bring the sugar and water solution to a boil. When it boils, reduce the heat and cook for 5–6 minutes until it turns into a golden caramel. Add half the salted popcorn to the pan, stir to mix evenly, then tip the popcorn out on to a large tray and allow to cool.

Opposite:
Salted spiced popcorn (left)
Caramel spiced popcorn (right)

MASALA CASHEW NUTS

There are several varieties of these spiced nuts available in supermarkets, but believe me – these ones are far superior. They're a great addition to garnish dishes or, if you're just plain greedy like me, enjoy them by the fistful with drinks!

SERVES 4

2 tablespoons corn oil
1 garlic clove, finely chopped
1 teaspoon cumin seeds
200g roasted salted cashew nuts, whole or split
½ teaspoon red chilli powder
1 teaspoon dried fenugreek leaves, crushed
1 teaspoon sugar
½ teaspoon Chaat Masala (see page 224)
1 tablespoon chopped coriander (optional)

Heat the oil in a frying pan, add the chopped garlic and cumin and cook over a medium heat until crisp. Add the cashew nuts, stir for 30 seconds or so, then add the remaining spices and sugar and mix well.

Remove from the heat and allow to cool to room temperature, then store in an airtight container. If using coriander, add just before serving.

ENTERTAINING

STICKY CHICKEN WINGS

Everyone loves chicken wings. I remember making hundreds of chicken lollipops (as we would call them) for the coffee-shop menu at The Oberoi in New Delhi. Those ones were coated in a spiced gram flour batter and deep-fried, but I find these ones better for entertaining at home as well as being healthy (well, relatively!). Serve either with a kachumber salad as a starter or on their own as a wonderfully messy snack.

SERVES 4

1kg chicken wings, skin on
1 teaspoon sea salt
50g coriander, chopped

For the marinade
1 tablespoon black peppercorns, coarsely cracked
4 garlic cloves, finely chopped
2 tablespoons grain mustard
juice of 2 lemons
3 tablespoons runny honey

For the kachumber salad
½ medium-sized cucumber, deseeded and finely diced
½ carrot, peeled and finely diced
1 medium-sized tomato, deseeded and finely diced
1 red onion, finely diced
½ green chilli, finely chopped
1 teaspoon chopped fresh coriander

For the salad dressing
juice of 1 lemon
1 teaspoon salt
½ teaspoon sugar

Mix the marinade ingredients together in a large, deep bowl. Add the chicken wings, mix well and set aside for at least an hour or overnight if possible.

Make the salad in a large bowl. Mix together all the ingredients for the dressing and gently fold in the vegetables.

Preheat oven to 200ºC/Gas Mark 6. Line a large baking tray with foil.

Place the chicken wings on the baking tray. Sprinkle with sea salt, and drizzle over half of the remaining marinade. Cook in the preheated oven for 35–40 minutes. Halfway through cooking, turn the chicken over and add the remaining marinade, cooking until the wings become sticky and coated. Just before removing the chicken wings from the oven, sprinkle over the coriander and stir in.

HONEY AND CHILLI POTATOES

I remember this dish as my wife Archana's favourite when we used to live in Jaipur and visit our favourite vegetarian Indo-Chinese restaurant, 4 Seasons. I'm sharing a recipe to make these from scratch but if you are in a rush, you could use frozen spiced potato wedges from the supermarket. These make an ideal party snack when you've raided everything else in the kitchen cupboard!

SERVES 2

450g new potatoes, boiled in the skin, peeled, cut in half and allowed to cool
2 garlic cloves, finely chopped
1 teaspoon red chilli flakes
2 teaspoons nigella seeds
1 teaspoon salt
50g cornflour
vegetable oil, for deep frying

For the sauce
1½ teaspoons vegetable oil
2 garlic cloves, chopped
1 teaspoon red chilli flakes
1 tablespoon sesame seeds
1 tablespoon tomato ketchup
2 teaspoons vinegar (rice, malt or white wine vinegar work well)
1½ tablespoons honey
1 teaspoon chopped coriander leaves (optional) or spring onion greens

Combine the peeled potatoes with garlic, red chilli flakes, nigella, salt and cornflour in a large bowl and set aside for 5 minutes.

Heat the oil in a deep-fat fryer to 180°C. Sprinkle the potatoes lightly with approximately 2 tablespoons of water to make the cornflour stick better to the potatoes. Deep fry in batches for 3–4 minutes until crisp and golden, then drain on kitchen paper and keep aside.

For the sauce, heat the oil in a separate pan or wok. Add the garlic and stir until it starts to turn golden, then add the chilli flakes, sesame seeds, ketchup, vinegar and honey and stir for a minute or so until mixed well and the sauce turns glossy.

Toss the fried potatoes in the sauce, sprinkle with coriander or spring onions and serve immediately.

CRAB FILO PARCELS WITH PLUM CHUTNEY

This is my version of a traditional patti or samosa. Crab, being a very delicate meat, is wrapped in a filo pastry and cooked to perfection. The plum chutney adds colour and flavour to the dish.

SERVES 4

2 tablespoons vegetable oil
1 teaspoon cumin seeds
2 onions, finely chopped
2.5cm piece of ginger, finely chopped
2 green chillies, chopped
1 teaspoon ground turmeric
200g crab meat (preferably white meat, but equal quantities of white and brown meat would be OK), pasteurised or cooked
2 teaspoons salt
½ teaspoon sugar
1 tablespoon chopped coriander
½ teaspoon garam masala
juice of ½ lemon
1 pack of 12 frozen filo pastry sheets or thin samosa sheets
40g butter, melted

For the plum chutney

1kg plums, stoned and roughly chopped
2 star anise
4 cardamom pods, bruised
1 teaspoon red chilli powder
200g sugar
200ml malt vinegar

To make the chutney, place the chopped plums in a pan with the star anise, cardamom pods, chilli powder, sugar and vinegar. Bring to a simmer and cook over a low heat for 25–30 minutes, stirring occasionally until the chutney coats the back of the spoon. Cool and set it aside in sterilized jars. This will make around 3 jars which will keep for up to 12 months. The chutney is quite vinegary to begin with, but mellows over time.

To cook the crab filling, heat the oil in a pan and add in the cumin and onions. Sauté for 5 minutes until the onions turn translucent. Stir in ginger, green chillies and turmeric. Fold in the crab meat and toss slowly. Sprinkle the salt and sugar onto the crab. Finish with chopped coriander, garam masala and lemon juice and set aside to cool.

To make the parcels, lay one filo sheet on the table and spread butter all over it with a brush. Place the second sheet on top of this buttered sheet and spread the top sheet with butter. Immediately cover it with the third and final sheet.

Using a sharp knife, divide these layered sheets into 4 strips, each 7cm wide. Place one strip on the work surface and brush its entire length with melted butter on the side facing you. Place 2 teaspoons of the crab mixture into one corner of the strip. Fold the filo over the mixture to form a triangle. Continue folding it until you reach the end of the strip. Seal the end with some melted butter if required. Repeat this procedure with the remaining strips, then repeat with the remaining sheets of pastry. You should end up with around 12 parcels in total.

Preheat oven to 220°C/Gas Mark 7. Place a baking tray in the oven to preheat.

Place the crab parcels on the preheated baking tray, brush with melted butter and bake for 8–10 minutes.

To serve, place the hot crab filo parcels on plates and pour some plum chutney around them.

Tip: Filo pastry is very delicate and has to be handled carefully. Keep it covered with kitchen paper or clingfilm while working as exposure to air will dry the filo and make it crisp. Alternatively, you can use samosa sheets.

GALOUTI KEBAB

This tender lamb kebab is famed for its melt-in-the-mouth texture, which is essentially down to using top-quality meat, then multiple stages of chilling and mincing. Here I suggest using mince instead of leg of lamb, then mixing all the other ingredients and chilling in a freezer for 30 minutes, and finally blending for a few seconds at a time in a food processor to get a fine mince texture. If you blend for a little longer, you can make a pâté that you can simply serve over brioche (cook in the same way as for the patties).

SERVES 6

4 tablespoons dried onions, fried (or thinly sliced onion fried until crisp)
2 tablespoons fried cashew nuts
500g lean lamb mince
3 tablespoons Ginger and Garlic Paste (see page 226)
1½ tablespoons red chilli powder
3 tablespoons ghee, melted
a pinch of saffron, soaked in 2 tablespoons of water
1 teaspoon pineapple juice
1½ teaspoons salt
4 drops of rose or kewra water (also known as screwpine essence, available from most Asian food stores or online)

For the spice mix
½ teaspoon cumin seeds, roasted and cooled
seeds of 4 green cardamom pods
1 blade of mace
seeds of 1 black cardamom pod
½ teaspoon black peppercorns
⅛ nutmeg
4 cloves

Mix together the fried onions and cashew nuts and blend to a smooth paste in a blender.

To make the spice mix, mix together all the spices and grind to a fine powder using a pestle and mortar.

Put the minced meat into a mixing bowl, add the spice mix and all the other ingredients except the ghee and rose water. Mix well with a spoon or spatula. Add two tablespoons of the ghee to the mixture, stir in well and chill in the freezer for 20–30 minutes.

Take the chilled mince out of the freezer and blend in a food processor, pulsing slowly at first and then for longer durations as the chilled mixture breaks down. Blend for 2–3 minutes until the mixture resembles fine mince. Add the remaining tablespoon of ghee and rose or kewra water, mix thoroughly and refrigerate again for 15–20 minutes.

Shape the minced meat into patties of about 40–50g each and 4cm in diameter and 1cm thick.

Heat a non-stick heavy-based frying pan and fry the patties over a low heat for 1–2 minutes on each side until they are well cooked (there's no need to add extra ghee to the pan). Remove from the pan and drain on kitchen paper. Serve hot with sheermal (see page 168), naan bread (see page 169) or even a slice of toasted brioche.

TANDOORI CHICKEN SPRING ROLLS

This is a particularly simple dish to make when entertaining friends, and combines two of the favourite foods for most Indian people – tandoori chicken and spring rolls. It's a good one to be prepared in advance so all that remains to be done is to fry the spring rolls when the guests arrive. Serve with an assortment of Green Coriander Chutney (see page 190), sweet chilli or Pineapple Dipping Sauce (see page 194).

MAKES 12-15

2 tablespoons vegetable oil, plus extra for deep-frying
3 garlic cloves, finely chopped
2.5cm piece of ginger or galangal, chopped
2 red onions, sliced lengthways
2 green onions, sliced into matchsticks
1 green or red chilli, finely chopped
40g cabbage, shredded or finely chopped
2 tablespoons soy sauce
2 tablespoons fish sauce (optional)
½ teaspoon salt
½ teaspoon sugar
300g cooked tandoori Chicken Tikka, finely chopped (see page 52)
80g bean sprouts
12–15 small spring roll wrapper sheets (thawed if frozen)
50g coriander, roughly chopped
40g basil, roughly chopped
2 tablespoons lime juice

Place the oil in a wok or large frying pan over a high heat. Add the garlic, ginger or galangal, onions and chilli. Stir-fry for 1 minute until fragrant, then add the cabbage and sauté briskly for 30 seconds or so. Add the sauces, salt and sugar. Stir-fry for 1–2 minutes, until the vegetables have softened. Remove from the heat. Allow to cool down, then add the chopped chicken and bean sprouts, tossing to mix in. Taste for salt, adding a little more fish or soy sauce if not seasoned enough.

To assemble the rolls, lay the spring roll wrappers on a clean work surface. Place one heaped tablespoon of filling on each wrapper (if using large wrappers, you will need more filling, so will make fewer spring rolls). Spread filling along the width of the wrapper and two-thirds of the way down the length. Sprinkle some of the fresh coriander and basil over the filling, and squeeze over the lime juice. Fold the left and right sides of wrapper over filling. Lift up the end nearest you and tuck over, rolling upwards. Secure by dipping your fingers in some water and wetting the end to 'paste' it closed.

To fry the spring rolls, pour oil in a wok or deep-sided frying pan to a depth of 2.5cm and place over a medium-high heat. If using a deep fat fryer, heat the oil to 160–170ºC.

When oil begins to form snake-like lines across the bottom of the pan, it is starting to heat up. To test it, dip one corner of a spring roll into the oil. If it begins to sizzle and cook, the oil is ready.

Using tongs, place spring rolls in the oil, frying them for about 1 minute on each side. The spring rolls are cooked when they turn light to medium golden-brown. You may need to cook them in batches and don't overcrowd the pan. Drain on kitchen paper while you carry on frying the rest. Serve hot.

CHILLI FISH ROLLS

Think hakka-style chilli fish, then think fish cakes, only smaller! These fish rolls, as we know them in Bengal, are like nothing you've tried before. Serve with tomato ketchup mixed with a little mustard.

SERVES 4
(AS A STARTER)

2 tablespoons vegetable oil, plus extra for deep frying
10 curry leaves (optional)
2 small red onions, thinly sliced
4 green chillies, thinly sliced
2.5cm piece of ginger, cut into small matchsticks
approximately 300g (1 large fillet) sea bass, sea bream or haddock, pinboned, skinned and diced into 2.5cm pieces
1 teaspoon red chilli flakes
½ teaspoon salt
a pinch of sugar
1 tablespoon dark soy sauce
2 tablespoons chopped coriander

For the mashed potatoes
500–600g potatoes
40g butter
½ teaspoon cumin seeds
¼ teaspoon ground turmeric
2.5cm piece of ginger, finely chopped
2 hot green chillies, finely chopped
½ teaspoon salt
2 teaspoons chopped coriander

For the coating
2 tablespoons flour
2 eggs
100g Japanese breadcrumbs

Boil the potatoes, then mash them and pass through a ricer to obtain a fine mash.

Heat the butter in a small pan, add the cumin seeds and let them crackle. Add the turmeric, ginger and green chilli and sauté for about 30 seconds. Add the salt, then pour onto the potatoes and mix well. Finally, add the coriander. You can add some more butter to give extra richness if you wish. Allow to cool, then divide into 12 equal sized balls.

For the fish, heat the oil in a wok over a high heat, then add the curry leaves, if using, and onions and sauté for 10 minutes until soft. Add the green chillies and ginger, then the diced fish and stir over a high heat for 2–3 minutes. Add the chilli flakes, salt, sugar and soy sauce and stir to mix well. Reduce the heat to medium, cover with a lid to let the fish cook in its steam for a couple of minutes, then remove the lid and increase the heat again. Check the seasoning. Flake the fish coarsely, sprinkle with coriander and set aside. When cool, divide into 12 balls and chill.

Hold one of the mashed potato balls in the palm of one hand, make a hole in the middle with a teaspoon, fill with some of the fish, then mould the potato round to enclose the fish. Repeat the process for all 12 balls, then dip in seasoned flour, egg and breadcrumbs.

Deep fry at 170ºC for 3–4 minutes until the croquettes are golden in colour (you may need to fry in batches), drain on kitchen paper and serve with a ketchup-mustard mix.

LAMB KEBAB SKEWERS WITH OYSTERS

An excellent cocktail snack, these will have your guests talking for weeks.

SERVES 4-6

12 fresh oysters, shucked
15cm piece of sugar cane, peeled and cut into 12 skewers 5mm thick (alternatively, use kebab sticks)

For the seekh kebab
500g minced lamb
70g lamb kidney fat (or any other fat, such as lard)
¼ teaspoon cumin seeds
2 green chillies, chopped
8 fresh coriander stems, chopped
3 garlic cloves, chopped
1cm piece of ginger, finely chopped
50g Cheddar cheese, grated
1 teaspoon red chilli powder
1 teaspoon salt

For the dressing
1 red onion, finely chopped
1 green chilli, finely chopped
½ ripe mango, peeled, stoned and chopped into 5mm dice
¼ cucumber peeled, seeded and chopped into 5mm dice
juice of ½ lemon
¼ teaspoon salt
½ teaspoon sugar

Mix all the kebab ingredients together in a food processor or by kneading with your hands, then chill in the fridge for 30 minutes. Divide the chilled mixture into 12 equal-sized kebabs, shaping them onto the sugar-cane skewers. Wet your hands before doing this to avoid the mince sticking.

Mix together all ingredients for the dressing, then chill in the fridge for 30 minutes.

Preheat the grill to medium hot.

Place the kebabs under the grill and cook for 8 minutes, rotating them so they become dark brown on all sides.

Pour the dressing over the freshly shucked oysters and serve alongside the lamb kebab skewers as cocktail snacks.

FISH AND SEAFOOD SKEWERS

These yakitori-style seafood skewers are great for entertaining.

MAKES 6
(OF EACH VERSION)

Prawns
12 small prawns, heads and shells removed
50ml olive oil
50ml soy sauce
1 tablespoon brown sugar
1 teaspoon fennel seeds, roasted and crushed

Salmon
300g salmon, cut into pieces approximately 7.5 x 2.5 x 2.5cm
2 tablespoons chopped coriander
zest of ½ lemon
1 red onion, finely chopped
1 tablespoon tamarind paste
½ teaspoon salt
½ teaspoon cracked black pepper

Scallops
6 scallops, cleaned and dried on kitchen paper
2 tablespoons sweet dark soy sauce
juice of 1 lime
1 tablespoon sesame seeds

Halibut/haddock/cod
400g fish fillet, cut into strips
150ml soy sauce
1 teaspoon ground cumin
1 teaspoon balsamic vinegar
1 tablespoon molasses or brown sugar

bamboo skewers, soaked in warm water for a couple of hours

Mix together the ingredients for the marinade of your choice. Marinate the fish or shellfish in its marinade for 5 minutes, then thread onto bamboo skewers.

Cook under a preheated grill or in a plancha grill, or on a barbecue, for approximately 5 minutes, turning on all sides to cook evenly. Serve immediately.

MEAT SKEWERS

These are a few skewer ideas which are great for entertaining and impressing your friends. Perfect for the barbecue as well as indoor entertaining, they do make life much easier, as the devil of preparation has been taken care of in advance. For skewers, use soaked bamboo skewers, twigs of rosemary or even thin sticks carved out of sugar cane, if you can find sugar cane in the shops.

MAKES 4-6 (OF EACH VERSION)

Duck breast

1 duck breast, sliced into 6 slivers
½ teaspoon salt
¼ teaspoon crushed chilli flakes
2 tablespoons tomato ketchup
2 tablespoons soy sauce
2 garlic cloves, finely grated
1 tablespoon molasses

Mix together all marinade ingredients, then add the duck and marinate for 5–10 minutes. Thread on to skewers. Cook under a preheated grill or cook in a griddle pan over a high heat for 3–5 minutes, turning, to cook on all sides. Serve immediately.

Chicken breast

2 chicken breasts, cut into 3 slices each
2 tablespoons cream cheese
1 teaspoon cracked black pepper
½ teaspoon salt
1 green chilli, finely chopped
2.5cm piece of ginger, finely chopped
1 tablespoon chopped coriander

Mix together all the marinade ingredients, then add the chicken and marinate for 15 minutes. Thread on to skewers. Cook under a preheated grill or cook in a griddle pan over a high heat for 3–5 minutes, turning, to cook on all sides. Check the chicken is cooked all the way through, then serve immediately.

Lamb seekh kebab

250g minced lamb
¼ teaspoon cumin seeds
2 green chillies, chopped
8 fresh coriander stems
2 garlic cloves
1cm piece of ginger, finely chopped
½ teaspoon red chilli powder
½ teaspoon salt

Mix all the ingredients together in a bowl, then divide into four equal-sized kebabs and use your hands to shape on to skewers. Wet your hands when doing this to avoid the mince sticking. Place under a preheated medium-hot grill, on a barbecue or in a grill pan for 8 minutes, turning them so they colour evenly to a dark brown on all sides.

Chicken liver and figs

6 dried figs
50ml dark rum
150g chicken livers, trimmed
1 teaspoon chilli flakes
1 teaspoon ground turmeric
½ teaspoon cumin seeds
½ teaspoon fennel seeds
2 garlic cloves, finely chopped
2 tablespoons vegetable oil
2 tablespoons sweet soy sauce
6 dried rosemary twigs, leaves removed and twigs soaked in water for a couple of hours

Soak the figs in the rum for 10 minutes. Marinate the chicken livers with all the remaining ingredients (apart from the rosemary twigs) for 10 minutes. Thread the livers and figs alternately on to the rosemary twigs and cook on a hot barbecue or preheated plancha grill (or under a preheated grill) for 5–6 minutes, turning halfway through the cooking time. Serve immediately.

TANDOORI CHICKEN PIZZA

For years I've served small paneer cheese pizzas on naan bread, called naanza, as canapés in our restaurants, but there is no reason why they have to be vegetarian. This version with tandoori chicken and chillies works well, and so does a variation with cooking pancetta. For a vegetarian version, use grilled mushrooms, sweetcorn or paneer cheese instead of the meat. Give it a go!

SERVES 4

2 tablespoons vegetable oil, ghee or butter
½ teaspoon cumin seeds
2 garlic cloves, chopped
1 onion, finely chopped
1 teaspoon chilli flakes
half a red pepper, finely diced
half a yellow pepper, finely diced
half a green pepper, finely diced
3 tomatoes, blended to purée
1½ teaspoons salt
2 green chillies, finely chopped
2 tablespoons single cream
1 tablespoon chopped coriander
juice of 1 lemon
4 naan breads – either try making your own (see page 169) or buy from a supermarket
½ quantity of tandoori-style Chicken Tikka (see page 52), sliced or chopped (if using diced pancetta, cook the pancetta as per packet instructions)

50g Cheddar or Parmesan cheese, grated

Heat the oil, ghee or butter in a heavy-based frying pan over a medium heat. Add the cumin seeds and when they start to crackle, add the garlic and sauté for 1 minute until golden. Add the onion and sauté for 3–4 minutes until it starts changing colour. Add the chilli flakes, salt and diced peppers and sauté for 5 minutes until they start turning soft.

Now add the tomatoes and cook for another 5–6 minutes. Add the salt, green chillies and cream and mix well. Sprinkle with coriander and lemon juice. Leave to cool.

Preheat the grill to medium.

Once the mixture has cooled down, spread the mix on the naan breads, sprinkle with chopped tandoori chicken or cooked pancetta, sprinkle with grated cheese and place under the preheated grill. Grill for 5–6 minutes until the edges of the naan become crisp and the cheese melts. Alternatively, Preheat oven to 160ºC/Gas Mark 4 and cook the naan for 10–12 minutes.

Cut into wedges and serve with a salad of your choice.

AMRITSAR-SPICED FISH FINGERS

Crisp, spicy, pungent and hot – that's how the Punjabis like their fried fish. I love their use of carom seed, chillies and garlic with fish. All are bold flavours, but you'll understand the reason why when you look at a map of Punjab. Miles away from the coast, most of the fish eaten are freshwater varieties, and often not the freshest. That said, the spicing works brilliantly on these fish fingers, which are great as snacks or to serve with drinks. If you have a deep fat fryer, this is an easy dish to prepare.

SERVES 4

600g white fish fillets, such as pollack, coley or cod, cut into finger-sized portions
vegetable oil or mustard oil (if you can handle it!), for deep frying
lemon wedges, to serve

For the marinade
3–4 garlic cloves, grated on a microplane
1 teaspoon salt
1 teaspoon red chilli powder
1 teaspoon carom seeds (also known as ajwan seeds)
juice of ½ lemon

For the batter
2½ tablespoons gram flour
4 tablespoons cornflour
½ teaspoon salt
½ teaspoon sugar
1½ teaspoons red chilli powder
½ teaspoon garam masala
2.5cm piece of ginger, finely chopped
1 tablespoon chopped coriander
juice of 1 lemon

Pat the fish fillets dry on kitchen paper.

Mix all the marinade ingredients together in a bowl, then add the fish and gently stir to coat. Set aside for 15 minutes.

Mix the batter ingredients together with 70ml water to a smooth and thick consistency.

Set your fryer to 170ºC. Dip the fish in the batter and fry in batches for 3–5 minutes until golden. Drain on kitchen paper.

Serve hot with Green Coriander Chutney (see page 190) or Mustard Aioli (see page 195) and lemon wedges.

CAULIFLOWER AND CUMIN SOUP

When cauliflower is prepared in our restaurant kitchens, I cringe whenever I see the stems, stalks and trimmings go to waste. We now make this simple but very effective soup and serve it as an *amuse bouche* every now and again. With or without the truffle oil it's a beauty.

SERVES 6

2 tablespoons vegetable oil
2 teaspoons cumin seeds
3 cloves
1 large white onion, coarsely chopped
1 large head of cauliflower (or stem, stalk, woody bits or leftovers from another recipe), cut into florets
1½ teaspoons salt
3 green chillies, slit lengthways
1 litre hot chicken/vegetable stock or water
50ml single cream
2 teaspoons truffle-flavoured extra-virgin olive oil (optional)

Heat the vegetable oil in a heavy-based pan and add the cumin and cloves. When the cumin crackles, add in the onion and sweat lightly for about 10 minutes until it is translucent. Add the cauliflower and the salt and sauté over a low heat for a minute without colouring. Add the chillies and sweat for another minute, then add the stock. Cover the pan with a lid and cook very slowly for about 25–30 minutes until the cauliflower is completely soft.

Blend the cauliflower using a stick blender while pouring in the cream. Check the seasoning and serve with crusty bread of your liking. Finish with a drizzle of truffle oil if using.

RAVIOLI OF PUMPKIN CHUTNEY WITH PUMPKIN SOUP

Making ravioli at home can take time but if you're up for it, it's a great way to get the kids involved in cooking. Here I use pumpkin chutney as a filling, but there is no set rule for the fillings – you could be more creative and, for example, use sautéed spinach with garlic and cumin, and fold it in the chutney.

SERVES 4

For the ravioli pasta dough
550g pasta flour
a generous pinch of salt
4 eggs
6 egg yolks
2 tablespoons olive oil
beaten egg, for brushing the pasta

For the pumpkin chutney
4 tablespoons vegetable oil
½ teaspoon fenugreek seeds
1 dried red chilli, broken into 2 or 3 pieces
500g pumpkin, diced into 1cm cubes
1½ teaspoons salt
½ teaspoon ground turmeric
1 tablespoon red chilli powder
5 tablespoons sugar
2 teaspoons dried amchoor (dried green mango powder) or mango pickle masala
1 tablespoon pine nuts, toasted

For the pumpkin soup
500g pumpkin, peeled and chopped into 2.5cm dice
2 large onions, roughly sliced
2 garlic cloves
2 tablespoons tamarind pulp (available in cans)
1 teaspoon red chilli powder
1 tablespoon vegetable oil
1 teaspoon mustard seeds
1 dried red chilli, broken into 2 or 3 pieces
8 curry leaves
2 teaspoons salt
1 teaspoon sugar
250ml coconut milk

To make the pasta dough, sift the flour and salt together and place in a large mixing bowl. Make a well in the middle and add the eggs, yolks and oil. Work on the dough slowly using a food processor or your hands first in the bowl, then transfer the mix to a floured work surface until the mixture starts to come together in coarse crumbs. Knead well until you have a smooth, firm ball of dough. It should feel soft but not sticky (if it is sticky, add a little extra flour). Wrap the dough in cling film and let it rest in the fridge for an hour or two.

Divide the dough ball into eight equal pieces and knead each piece again until smooth. Taking a piece at a time, roll out each one in turn with a rolling pin on a lightly floured board until you have a rectangle about 5mm thick.

Feed each rectangle of dough through the pasta machine several times starting with the mechanism adjusted to the thickest setting (i.e. with the rollers widest apart) and adjusting the setting by one notch each time, finishing with the thinnest setting. You should have rectangle sheets approximately 7.5 cm wide and as thin as you possibly can get. Dust with dry flour to prevent them sticking together, cover with clingfilm and keep aside until you are ready to fill the raviolis.

To make the pumpkin chutney, heat the oil in a pan over a high heat. Add the fenugreek seeds and dried red chilli and let them pop. Add the diced pumpkin and stir over a high heat for 3–4 minutes. Stir in the salt, turmeric, and chilli powder, then reduce the heat, cover and cook for about 10 minutes until the pumpkin is soft. Stir in the sugar. If necessary, mash a little, using a spoon, to make a rough purée. Finish with the toasted pine nuts. Set aside to cool before using to fill the ravioli.

Trim the pasta sheets to 7.5cm width, then lay one sheet on a floured surface. Spoon tablespoons of pumpkin chutney on to the sheet, placing them approximately 7.5cm apart. Using a brush, apply egg around the chutney lightly. Lay the second sheet of pasta over

the pumpkin carefully, pressing around the chutney with your fingers to seal the edges and rid of any air pockets. Cut the ravioli into 7.5cm squares and keep covered with clingfilm until you are ready to cook.

Preheat oven to 180°C/Gas Mark 4.

To make the pumpkin soup, mix together the diced pumpkin, onions, garlic, tamarind pulp and red chilli powder, and drizzle with a splash of water. Tip the mixture onto a baking tray, cover with foil and bake in the oven for 20–30 minutes. Remove from the oven when soft and blend into a smooth purée.

Heat the oil in a pan, add the mustard seeds, dried red chillies and curry leaves and cook for a few seconds over a high heat. Remove and discard the chillies, then add the pumpkin purée, salt and sugar. Adjust to a soup consistency by adding 300–400ml water. Add the coconut milk in the end.

Cook the ravioli in boiling salted water for 2 minutes. Serve the ravioli floating in the pumpkin soup.

ENTERTAINING

TOM KHA GAI THAI SOUP

I know this isn't Indian nor will I say I grew up drinking Thai soup at home, but when I joined the Oberoi Hotel in New Delhi in 1993, the Thai restaurant there was one of the first kitchens where my training began. It was this soup that was my first introduction to the wonderfully fragrant, hot, sour and fresh world of Thai cuisine. It still remains one of my favourite things to eat. I make it frequently at home, and hope you will love it too.

SERVES 4

750ml low-salt chicken stock
a pinch of ground turmeric
2 stalks of lemongrass
5–6 fresh bird's eye chillies, slit lengthways
4–5 fresh kaffir lime leaves
400g tin of full-fat coconut milk
5cm piece of fresh galangal (or ginger), thinly sliced
225g fresh oyster mushrooms, cut into bite-sized pieces
450g boneless, skinless chicken breasts, sliced 3–5mm thick across the grain
juice of 2–3 limes
60ml fish sauce
a small bunch of coriander, coarsely torn

First, concentrate the stock. Put the chicken stock in a wide, shallow saucepan with the turmeric. Bring to the boil, then reduce it over medium-high heat until the liquid measures half its original volume.

Cut the lemongrass stalks into 2.5cm pieces and bruise them with the side of a pestle, or a similar heavy utensil. Bruise the slit chillies in a similar way.

Remove the stems and the tough veins that run through the middle of the kaffir lime leaves. Tear the leaves into 3–4 pieces and set aside.

Put the coconut milk into a large pan, followed by concentrated chicken stock, kaffir lime leaves, lemongrass pieces and galangal slices. Bring the mixture slowly almost to a simmer for about a minute. Keeping the temperature steady, add the mushrooms and the chicken to the liquid; adjust the heat to maintain a steady simmer. The liquid should never reach a rapid boil. Stir gently for 5–6 minutes to ensure that the chicken is evenly cooked. Add more liquid if needed – you are aiming for a soupy consistency, not a sauce.

Once the chicken is cooked through, add the smashed chillies and remove the pan from the heat immediately.

Add the juice of 2 limes and the fish sauce to the pan, stir and taste. Add more lime juice and fish sauce, as necessary. The soup should taste predominantly sour, followed by salty. The sweetness comes from natural sugar in the coconut milk.

Stir in the coriander leaves and serve your tom kha gai with steamed jasmine rice on the side as a main course.

RABBIT TIKKA

Rabbit and hare are considered delicacies in India. The mustard and honey marinade for this dish helps to seal in the flavours of the rabbit and the two strong flavours complement the taste of the meat. This would be an ideal barbecue dish as the smokiness from the charcoal brings out the best of this marinade. The papaya is used as a tenderiser. This dish also works well as a canapé with drinks.

SERVES 4
(AS A STARTER)

500g rabbit legs, deboned and cut into 2.5cm dice
8 bamboo skewers, soaked in water

For the first marinade
1 tablespoon Ginger and Garlic Paste (see page 226)
½ teaspoon red chilli powder
1 teaspoon ground turmeric
1 teaspoon salt
juice of 1 lemon
2.5cm piece of green papaya, finely grated (alternatively use 2 tablespoons of fresh pineapple juice or grated fresh pineapple

For the second marinade
100ml Greek yoghurt
2 tablespoons wholegrain mustard
1 tablespoon honey
1 teaspoon garam masala
2 green chillies, finely chopped

1 tablespoon chopped coriander
2 tablespoons mustard oil (alternatively use vegetable oil mixed with 1 teaspoon English mustard)

Mix together all the ingredients for the first marinade and rub onto the rabbit legs. Set aside in the fridge for 1 hour.

Mix together all the ingredients for the second marinade and apply to the rabbit. Leave for another hour or so in the fridge.

Thread the rabbit pieces onto skewers and cook on a hot barbecue for 10–15 minutes, turning regularly. Alternatively, Preheat oven to 180ºC/ Gas Mark 4, place the rabbit skewers on a baking tray and cook in the oven for 18–20 minutes, turning them regularly. If the rabbit cooks but does not take colour, place under a very hot grill for a couple of minutes.

Serve with Green Coriander Chutney (see page 190).

FUSION FISH CAKE

I picked up this recipe for fish cakes during my time in Baan Thai, the Thai restaurant at the Oberoi in New Delhi. Over the years I have forgotten which bits of other influences have crept in, and now it's a right fusion of Thai and Indian!

SERVES 4

100g skinless salmon or mackerel fillet, chopped
100g skinless white fish fillet (such as cod, coley, bass or bream), chopped
175g squid, chopped
2 red chillies, fresh or dried, deseeded and finely chopped
2 fresh green chillies, finely chopped with seeds
4 lime leaves, fresh or frozen, shredded
2.5cm piece of ginger, finely chopped
2 tablespoons chopped coriander, stems and leaves
1 red onion, finely chopped
50g green beans, trimmed and finely chopped
1 teaspoon salt
1 egg white
1 tablespoon oyster sauce (optional)
groundnut or vegetable oil, for deep frying

For the chilli dipping sauce
3 tablespoons fish sauce
3 tablespoons rice vinegar
5 tablespoons caster sugar
5cm piece of ginger, finely chopped
juice of 2 limes
3 large hot chillies, red or green, finely chopped
1 tablespoon light soy sauce

To serve
¼ cucumber, chopped into 5mm dice
25g roasted peanuts, chopped
2 tablespoons crisp fried onions

To make the dipping sauce, put the fish sauce, vinegar and sugar in a small saucepan with 6 tablespoons of water and bring to the boil. Crush the ginger to a pulp with the flat of the blade. Add the ginger to the pan and let the mixture boil for 2–3 minutes until it starts to thicken slightly. Let it cool, then add the lime, chillies and soy sauce.

Put the salmon, white fish and half of the squid into a food processor, then whizz until smooth. Add the chillies and pulse for another two or three times until mixed. Place all the other ingredients, including the remaining chopped squid but except the oil, into a large bowl. Add the fish mixture, then knead and mix together using your hands for 5 minutes until smooth and elastic.

Shape into small flat discs about 5cm across. Heat some oil in a wok or frying pan until it shimmers, then shallow fry the fish cakes in batches for 2–3 minutes on each side until golden. Drain on kitchen paper. Serve the fishcakes with the dipping sauce and the cucumber dice, chopped peanuts and crisp fried onions.

RICE, CUCUMBER AND CHICKEN SALAD

This is a great salad for a hot summer's day as it is simple and quick to prepare. You can substitute pork for chicken if you wish. It works just as well. If you want to sprout your own mung beans, soak whole moong beans overnight, then spread the soaked lentils in a germinator and let germinate. It may take 2–3 days, depending on how cold or warm your kitchen is.

SERVES 2

1 tablespoon raw basmati rice
½ a small cucumber
50g cooked basmati rice
   (20g uncooked weight)
2 large chicken breasts
2 tablespoons groundnut or vegetable
   oil
60g young spinach leaves
1 head of endive, cos or romaine
   lettuce, leaves separated, washed,
   dried and chilled
10 basil leaves, torn
2 large handfuls of sprouting mung
   beans
salt and pepper

For the dressing
2 garlic cloves, crushed or very finely
   chopped
2 small, hot red chillies
4 tablespoons lime juice
2 tablespoons fish sauce
1 teaspoon sugar

First roast the rice. Heat a dry frying pan, add the raw basmati rice and roast until the grains turn golden. Remove from the heat and allow to cool, then pound coarsely in a pestle and mortar. Keep aside.

Make the dressing. Put the garlic in a small bowl. Cut the chilli in half along its length, scrape out the seeds with a knife and discard, then slice the chilli thinly. Add it to the garlic. Squeeze in the lime juice, add the fish sauce and the sugar. Mix it briefly with a fork or small whisk.

Peel the cucumber, slice it thinly and toss gently with cooked rice and half the dressing. Set aside for 5–6 minutes in the fridge.

Preheat the grill or a griddle pan. Season the chicken with salt and pepper and rub or brush with groundnut or vegetable oil. Place under a hot grill or in a griddle pan and cook for 8–10 minutes until the skin is golden and the juices run clear.

Let the chicken rest for 5 minutes, then slice thickly and allow to cool. You should get four or five thick pieces from each breast. Place the marinated cucumber on a plate, scatter over the leaves and basil, add the cold chicken and then the sprouts. Pour over the remaining dressing. Sprinkle lightly with the pounded roasted rice and serve.

CAULIFLOWER AND SCALLOP STIR-FRY

This recipe is an example of how my home cooking differs from my mother's! Years of restaurant cooking has ensured that cheffy flourishes like purées, truffle and garnishes have crept into our home repertoire and sit next to my mother's cauliflower *bhujia*. Most of this dish can be done in advance and only the scallops need to be cooked at the last minute.

SERVES 4

For the truffled cauliflower purée
1 tablespoon vegetable oil
½ teaspoon cumin seeds
2 cloves
1 white onion, finely chopped (half is used for the purée and half in the stir-fry)
100g cauliflower offcuts (ie leftovers from the cauliflower used in the stir-fry), chopped
1 teaspoon salt
100ml chicken or vegetable stock or water
30ml single cream
10ml truffle-flavoured extra virgin olive oil

For the cauliflower stir-fry
2 tablespoons vegetable oil
1 teaspoon black onion seeds
1 teaspoon black cumin seeds
1 head of cauliflower, cut into 1cm florets, discard any stem or woody bits (reserve them for the purée)
½ teaspoon ground turmeric
1 teaspoon salt
½ teaspoon sugar
2.5cm piece of ginger, finely chopped
1 green chilli, finely chopped
1 tablespoon white wine vinegar
40g shelled peas

For the scallops
1 tablespoon vegetable oil
12 large scallops, wiped dry on kitchen paper
sea salt, to sprinkle
1 teaspoon chilli flakes
1 teaspoon fennel seeds
½ teaspoon sugar

To make the purée sauce, heat the oil in a heavy-based pan and add the cumin and cloves. When the cumin starts to crackle, add the onion and sweat lightly until it is translucent, then add the cauliflower and salt and sauté over a low heat for a minute without colouring. Pour in the chicken stock. Cover the pan with a lid and cook very slowly for about 15 minutes until most of the chicken stock has been absorbed by the cauliflower and it is absolutely soft. Blend the cauliflower in a blender, slowly adding the cream until it becomes light and smooth. Return the purée to the pan and keep warm over a very gentle heat. Just before serving, fold in the truffle oil and mix it lightly, then check the seasoning.

For the cauliflower stir-fry, heat the oil in a wide frying pan which has a lid. Add the black onion and cumin seeds. When they start to crackle, add the remaining chopped onion and sauté, stirring constantly, for 4–5 minutes until the onions are soft. Add the cauliflower and stir over a high heat for a minute or so, then add the turmeric, salt, sugar, ginger and chilli and stir to mix. Add the vinegar, reduce the heat and cover with a lid. Cook for a couple more minutes until the cauliflower florets are cooked but still crunchy. Stir in the peas and cover with a lid. Remove from the heat and keep warm.

To cook the scallops, heat the oil in a heavy-based frying pan until very hot, add the scallops and sear for 1-2 minutes until they form a caramelised crust on the bottom. While the scallops are cooking, sprinkle the raw side with sea salt, chilli flakes, fennel seeds and sugar, then turn the scallops over and cook on the second side for another 1–2 minutes until caramelised. You may sprinkle more seeds and seasoning if you wish on the other side. Drain the cooked scallops on a kitchen paper.

To assemble, place a couple spoonfuls of sauce on the plate, then sit the cauliflower stir-fry on top. Finish with the cooked scallops and serve immediately.

THAI-SPICED GRILLED SARDINES

Sardines are a good fish for grilling or barbecuing, and I especially like the Thai flavours here. The dip is an excellent addition, too, and would work just as well with satays or other poultry skewers.

SERVES 4

16–20 whole sardines, gutted and cleaned, skin slashed
1 tablespoon vegetable or olive oil

For the barbecue rub
2 teaspoons ground garlic
1½ teaspoons turmeric
1 teaspoon dried crushed chilli or ¾ teaspoon cayenne pepper
¼ teaspoon freshly ground black pepper
1 teaspoon nigella seeds
2 teaspoons salt
1 tablespoon cornflour

For the sauce
4 tablespoons vegetable or olive oil
2 tablespoons coconut milk or butter
2 fresh red chillies, deseeded and finely chopped, or ½ teaspoon dried crushed chilli or cayenne pepper
a bunch of coriander, chopped
3 tablespoons fish sauce
juice of 4 limes
4 garlic cloves, finely chopped
2 teaspoons brown sugar

Lightly oil a grill rack with a little cooking oil to prevent the fish sticking.

To make the barbecue rub, simply stir all the rub ingredients together in a small bowl.

Place prepared sardines on a tray or in a long casserole dish large enough for them to lie flat. Drizzle with 1 tablespoon of the vegetable oil and rub it evenly over the fish. Sprinkle the barbecue rub over the entire surface of the fish. Gently rub it along each fish, so they appear yellowy gold. Set aside to marinate until your barbecue/grill is hot.

Grill the fish for about 5–6 minutes on each side until cooked and the skin crisp.

To make the sauce, simply place all the sauce ingredients in a small pan. Warm over a medium heat for 2–3 minutes to bring out the flavours, taking care not to let the mixture boil. The sauce may separate, but that's OK. Adjust consistency, adding more fish sauce if not salty enough, or another squeeze of lime juice if too salty for your taste. Add a little more sugar if too sour.

To serve, spoon the sauce over the grilled fish. The sauce is very nice with rice too.

MURGH MAKHANI RAVIOLI

I find this recipe is a great way of using up leftover Butter Chicken (see page 102). The garnish of fried sage and truffle oil simply jazzes up the effort, but is by no means essential.

SERVES 4

For the filling
300g cooked tandoori Chicken Tikka (see page 52) or leftover Butter Chicken (see page 102), meat shredded or chopped into 5mm dice
1 small red onion, finely chopped
25g Parmesan or other hard Italian cheese, finely grated, plus extra to serve
180ml makhani sauce
sea salt flakes
freshly ground black pepper

For the makhani sauce
5 large tomatoes
1cm piece of ginger, crushed
1 clove of garlic, peeled
2 green cardamom pods
2 cloves
1 bay leaf
1 teaspoon red chilli powder
50ml single cream
¼ teaspoon garam masala
¼ teaspoon fenugreek leaves, dried and powdered
30g butter, diced and cooled
½ level teaspoon salt
1 teaspoon sugar

For the pasta
300g '00' grade flour, plus extra for dusting
3 large eggs
1 teaspoon salt

To garnish
2 tablespoons olive oil or truffle-flavoured olive oil
a handful of fresh sage leaves
4 sun-dried tomatoes, drained and cut into thin strips

For the sauce, wash and cut the tomatoes into halves, place them in a sauce pan with 100ml water. Add the ginger, garlic, cardamom, cloves and bay leaf. Bring to the boil, then reduce the heat and simmer for 15–20 minutes until the tomatoes are completely cooked and disintegrated. Pass through a sieve to get a fine tomato purée.

Boil the tomato purée and add the chilli powder. Cook for 2–3 minutes. As the sauce becomes a spoon-coating consistency, add the cream, simmer for 2 minutes, then add the garam masala and crushed fenugreek leaves. Allow to infuse for a minute and stir in the cold butter. If required, balance the sauce with the sugar.

For the filling, mix the chicken with the red onion and cheese, season with salt and pepper, then mix with 2–3 tablespoons of makhani sauce to moisten the mix. Set aside.

To make the pasta, blend the flour and eggs in a food processor until the ingredients come together to form a dough. Continue to pulse for a further minute, removing the lid and turning the dough over every 15–20 seconds. Turn the dough out onto a lightly floured surface and knead well for 10 minutes, pummelling and stretching the dough until it is smooth, stretchy and has a slight sheen. Divide the dough into four portions and wrap each in cling film. Chill in the fridge for 30 minutes.

When the pasta dough has chilled, take the first portion and roll it out onto a lightly floured work surface to a thickness of 1mm, dusting the dough with a light coating of flour if it starts to stick. You need the surface area of the rolled-out dough to yield 12 discs, each 8.5cm in diameter. Using an 8.5cm cookie cutter, gently mark 12 circles in the sheet of pasta dough, but without cutting through the dough.

Repeat the rolling-out process with the second portion of pasta dough, but do not mark with the cookie cutter. Set aside carefully.

Divide the filling mixture in half and place one heaped teaspoon into the centre of each marked pasta disc. Brush the dough surrounding the filling with a little cold water.

Once all the discs have been filled, lift the second sheet of pasta dough and drape it over the first, carefully smoothing the pasta around the mounds of filling. Use your fingertips to remove any air bubbles and stick the moistened sheets of pasta together. Dust a baking tray with a little flour. Use the same cookie cutter to cut out the 12 ravioli, then place each on the prepared baking tray. Set aside until needed.

Repeat the process with the remaining pasta and filling mixture to make 12 more ravioli.

For the garnish, heat the olive oil in a small frying pan over a medium-high heat. Add the sage leaves and fry for 10–15 seconds, or until they look translucent. Remove from the pan using a slotted spoon and set aside to drain on kitchen paper. Return the pan to the heat and add the sun-dried tomatoes. Fry for 20–30 seconds, stirring well, until heated through. Add the makhani sauce and heat through. Remove from the heat and set aside.

To cook the ravioli, half fill a very large saucepan with cold water. Add the salt and bring to the boil. When the water is boiling, carefully lower in the ravioli, in batches if necessary, using a slotted spoon. Boil for 3–5 minutes, until the pasta is cooked to your liking. (To test the cooking time, boil a few of the trimmings to check how long they need.)

Carefully drain the ravioli in a colander and return to the saucepan. Stir in the sun-dried tomatoes and sauce. Season to taste with salt and freshly ground black pepper.

To serve, divide the ravioli among four warmed plates, spooning over any sun-dried tomatoes left in the saucepan. Garnish with the fried sage leaves and sprinkle over a little cheese. Drizzle with truffle-flavoured olive oil and serve immediately.

KERALA-SPICED SEAFOOD LINGUINE

Yes, pasta isn't native to Kerala but this sauce and its spicing are brilliant with pasta. The flavours are alive and kicking, and this is quite simply one of my favourite things to eat.

SERVES 3-4

300g linguine pasta
200g sugar snap peas, trimmed
2 tablespoons corn or vegetable oil
1 teaspoon black mustard seeds
12–15 curry leaves
2 large garlic cloves, finely chopped
1 large red chilli, seeded and finely chopped
1 large onion, finely chopped
1 teaspoon salt
½ teaspoon sugar
1½ teaspoons red chilli powder
2 tomatoes, finely chopped
2.5cm piece of ginger, finely chopped
1 tablespoon kokum or tamarind (optional)
60ml coconut milk
500g raw king prawns, peeled (if peeling them yourself, you will need to start with approximately 750g)
a handful of basil leaves
½ teaspoon cracked black pepper
½ teaspoon dried red chilli flakes
sea salt flakes (optional)

Cook the pasta in a pan of boiling water, according to the instructions on the pack. Add the sugar snap peas for the last minute or so of cooking time. Drain and reserve.

Meanwhile, heat the oil in a wok or large frying pan, add the mustard seeds and curry leaves and allow to crackle and pop. Toss in the garlic and chopped red chilli and cook over a fairly high heat for about 30 seconds without letting the garlic brown.

Once the garlic has softened, add the onion and sauté over a high heat for 5 minutes or so until the onions start to change colour. Add the salt, sugar and chilli powder, stir to mix well, then add the tomatoes and cook another 4–5 minutes until the moisture is absorbed and mixture starts to turn glossy. Add the ginger, kokum or tamarind, if using, and the coconut milk and mix well.

Tip in the prawns and cook over a high heat, stirring frequently, for about 3–4 minutes until they turn translucent and pink.

Toss the pasta and sugar snaps into the prawn mixture. Tear in the basil leaves, stir, and season with pepper and chilli flakes. Check the seasoning; if adding salt, use sea salt flakes.

BANGLA FISH PIE

I made a Kerala-spiced seafood pie on *Saturday Kitchen* a few years ago, and it was so good it became a fixture on our Cinnamon Soho menu. This Bengali-spiced version makes an excellent one-dish meal for the family. The spicing differs from the dish I cooked on television, and whereas the original was pastry-encased this one is topped with mash.

SERVES 6

2 tablespoons vegetable or corn oil
4 cloves
1 teaspoon carom seeds
2 bay leaves
1 small onion, finely chopped
1 teaspoon salt
4 green chillies, slit lengthways
400g skinless white fish fillet
400g skinless smoked haddock fillet
400ml tin of thick coconut milk
200ml fish stock or water
4 eggs
a small bunch of coriander, chopped

For the sauce
25g butter
25g flour
½ teaspoon turmeric
1 teaspoon chilli flakes
1½ tablespoons grain mustard

For the topping
1kg floury potatoes, peeled and cut into even chunks
25g butter

a pinch of freshly grated nutmeg
2 cooked beetroot, cut into sticks

Heat the oil in a wide frying pan (you'll need one large enough to accommodate the fillets in a single layer), then add the cloves, carom seeds and bay leaves and let them crackle and pop. Add the onion and sauté for 2–3 minutes, then add the salt and green chillies and place the fish fillets on top.

Pour over the thick coconut milk and fish stock. Reduce the heat, cover and poach the fish by bringing the liquid just to the boil (you will see a few small bubbles) and then simmering for 6–8 minutes, until the fish turns opaque and firm and would flake when pressed.

Lift the fish onto a plate. Pour the cooking liquid into a jug and allow to cool (you will need this for the sauce). When the fish is cool enough to touch, flake into large pieces in a baking dish.

Hard-boil the eggs. Bring a small pan of water to a gentle boil, then carefully lower the eggs in with a slotted spoon. Bring the water back to a gentle boil, cook for 8 minutes, then drain and cool in a bowl of cold water. Peel, slice into quarters and arrange on top of the fish, then scatter over the chopped coriander.

To make the sauce, melt the butter in a pan. Add the flour, turmeric and chilli flakes and cook for a minute, then add the reserved cooking liquid with spices, adding a little at a time, stirring to prevent lumps forming. Add the grain mustard and cook gently until the sauce coats the back of a spoon. Remove from the heat, correct the seasoning, then pour over the fish.

Preheat oven to 200°C/Gas Mark 6.

Boil the potatoes in a large pan of water for 20 minutes. Drain, season and mash with the butter and nutmeg. Use to top the pie – starting at the edge of the dish and working your way in, pushing the mash right to the edges to seal. Fluff the top with a fork, then stick the beetroot sticks in at equal intervals so that they are visible from the top. Bake for 30 minutes.

You can make this up to a day ahead. Refrigerate, then bake for 40 minutes.

Variations
If you wish, add 200g raw peeled king prawns to the baking dish along with the poached fish or simply scatter a handful of petits pois or peas into the pie before topping with the mash.

BAKED WHOLE FISH

This is a simple but very effective dish for entertaining or an impressive family lunch. You could easily wrap the fish in foil and cook over a barbecue, but baking in the oven is possibly the simplest method. I like sea bream a lot, but you can also use sea bass, pomfret, snapper or mackerel – anything you like really. The spice crust has quite a kick to it. Depending upon how coarsely you've pounded the spices, you end up with an interesting texture which beautifully highlights the delicate texture of moist fish.

SERVES 4

4 whole sea bream, 350–400g each, gutted, cleaned, fins and tail trimmed
1 tablespoon salt
1 tablespoon red chilli powder
2 teaspoons turmeric
juice of 2 lemons
4 tablespoons clarified butter, to baste
lemon wedges, to serve

For the stuffing (optional)
2 lime leaves, torn into 2–3 pieces
100g boiled basmati rice (30g uncooked weight)
zest of 2 lemons
1 teaspoon sugar

For the spice crust
4 tablespoons coriander seeds, roasted
4 tablespoons cumin seeds, roasted

2 teaspoons black peppercorns, roasted lightly
1 tablespoon red chilli powder
2 teaspoons salt
2 teaspoons sugar
6 garlic cloves, finely chopped
5cm piece of ginger, finely chopped
100g coriander stalks and leaves, finely chopped
4 tablespoons vegetable or corn oil

Using a sharp knife, slash the fish two or three times on each side and rub in the salt, chilli powder, turmeric and lemon juice. Set aside for 30 minutes.

Preheat oven to 200ºC/Gas Mark 6.

Mix together the stuffing ingredients and divide equally between the fish, spooning it into the belly. (You may omit the stuffing if you wish.)

To make the spice crust, coarsely pound all the dry ingredients together using a pestle and mortar, then mix together with the garlic, ginger, coriander and oil. Apply the spice crust to both sides of the fish to form an even coating.

Place the fish on a baking tray and cook in the preheated oven for 15–18 minutes. If the fish start to colour too quickly, reduce the temperature to 180ºC/Gas Mark 4 after 6–8 minutes and carefully turn the fish over for even cooking. Baste

with clarified butter halfway through the cooking time. If you think the spice crust is in danger of burning, cover the fish with foil. To check the fish is cooked, insert the tip of a sharp knife or a wooden skewer through the thickest part of the fish; if the juices run clear and the tip feels warm to the lips then the fish is cooked.

Serve the fish with a simple salad, accompanied by lemon wedges.

SPICE-ROASTED WHOLE CHICKEN

A good roast chicken is the king of all dishes, and most of the time it's a good test of a chef's skills. Like most good roasts, this version benefits from a good rest before serving.

SERVES 4

1.35–2.25kg roasting chicken
3 tablespoons salted butter, softened
2 lemons
1 teaspoon coarse sea salt
1 teaspoon chilli flakes
1 tablespoon coriander seeds, lightly crushed
50g basil or mint, chopped
75g coriander, leaves and stalks chopped
2 sprigs of thyme, chopped
2 heads of garlic, cut in half crosswise
1 tablespoon extra-virgin olive oil
2 tomatoes, cut in half
salt and freshly ground black pepper

For the sauce
60ml dry white wine
800ml homemade chicken stock
2 tablespoons double cream (optional)

Preheat oven to 230ºC/Gas Mark 8.

Pull any loose fat from around the chicken opening. Rub the outside of the bird with 1 tablespoon of the softened butter. Mix the remaining butter with the zest of 1 lemon, spices and half of the herbs. Rub the butter on the inside of the cavity and under the breast skin, taking care not to rip the skin. Sprinkle the inside and outside of the bird with the salt and pepper. Pierce the whole lemon with a sharp knife and put it in the cavity of the chicken.

For the crispiest skin, use a V-shaped rack, set in a heavy roasting pan just larger than the rack. Put the chicken, breast side up, on the rack. Cut the zested lemon in half and squeeze both halves over the chicken. Roast the chicken in the preheated oven for 15–20 minutes, then reduce the heat to 190ºC/Gas Mark 5.

Brush the garlic halves liberally with the olive oil, then add with the tomato halves to the roasting pan (place them near the chicken), and continue roasting for a further 45 minutes (a total of about 1 hour for a 1.35kg chicken; for larger birds, add another 10 minutes for each additional 500g). The chicken is done when the legs wiggle freely in their joints and the juices run clear from the thigh when pricked and from the cavity when you tilt the bird. If using a thermometer, insert into the lower meaty part of the thigh and it should register 76°C. Set the chicken on a warm platter, propping up the hindquarters with an inverted saucer, to drain out the juices. Tent with foil to keep it warm while you make the sauce.

Make the sauce from the pan drippings. Remove the rack from the pan, then tilt the pan and spoon off as much fat as possible. The garlic can either be transferred to the chicken platter, or incorporated into the sauce. Set the pan over a high heat to caramelise all the juices, mash up the tomatoes (and garlic, if using) as much as possible (be careful not to let them burn). Deglaze with wine, scraping up all drippings, and pass through a sieve into a saucepan. Boil until the liquid is a syrupy glaze, add about half the stock, and boil it down to a sputtering, bubbling glaze, about 5–8 minutes. Repeat with the remaining stock, boiling it down until reduced to about 150ml, about 5 minutes. Add the remaining herbs and cream, if using, taste, and adjust the seasoning.

Carve the chicken and serve the meat drizzled with some sauce and with the roasted garlic on the side or in the sauce as you prefer. Serve with rice or crusty bread.

RAAN

The grandest of Indian dishes, this is lamb curry but not as we know it. It combines two cooking techniques – braising and roasting – and the result is highly impressive. Although the recipe calls for lamb, feel free to use hogget, mutton or even goat.

SERVES 8-10

2 legs of lamb, weighing about 1.5kg each (bone in weight), trimmed of any surface fat
6 bay leaves
3 cinnamon sticks, about 5cm each, split
5 green cardamom pods
1.5 litres chicken stock or water, for braising
2 tablespoons butter, melted
2 teaspoons lemon juice
1 teaspoon Chaat Masala (see page 224)
4 tablespoons single cream
1 teaspoon Garam Masala (see page 225)
a pinch of saffron, soaked in a little warm water to soften
1 tablespoon chopped coriander
edible gold leaf, for decorating (optional)

For the marinade
2 tablespoons red chilli powder
5 tablespoons ginger paste (see page 226)
6 tablespoons garlic paste (see page 226)
250ml malt vinegar
500g plain yoghurt
3 large white onions, sliced and deep fried until crisp
2 teaspoons black cumin seeds
1 tablespoon salt

Using the tip of a sharp knife, cut small incisions in the legs of lamb at approximately 5cm intervals. Mix together the marinade ingredients, then massage them over the lamb, rubbing and pressing the spices into the gashes created by the knife. Set aside for at least 15 minutes, or longer if you have time (marinating overnight or for a few hours in the fridge would be fine).

Preheat oven to 180ºC/Gas Mark 4.

Put the legs and all marinade in an oiled roasting tin. Add the bay leaves, cinnamon and green cardamom. Add the chicken stock or water – you need enough to come about half way up the sides of the lamb. Cover the tray with foil.

Place in the preheated oven and braise for 2½ hours, turning it over in the marinade halfway through, until the meat is very tender and ready to fall of the bone (if it isn't tender after this time, cook for a little longer).

Remove from the oven, lift the lamb from the liquid, pat dry with kitchen paper and leave to cool. Pass the cooking juices through a fine sieve and reserve to make the sauce.

Take the meat off the bone and cut into 5cm cubes. Thread the cubes onto 8–10 metal skewers and roast on a barbecue or under a very hot grill for 8–10 minutes, turning and basting frequently with the melted butter, until crisp and well browned. Finish with a drizzle of lemon juice, any leftover melted butter and the chaat masala.

For the sauce, bring the cooking juices to the boil in a small pan and simmer until reduced to a coating consistency. Correct the seasoning and stir in the cream, garam masala, saffron and chopped coriander. Pour the sauce over the meat, sprinkle edible gold leaves if you wish and serve with naan bread (see page 169).

Tip
Do not throw away any scraps or leftover meat. It makes an excellent naan filling when stir-fried with red onions, peppers, chilli, etc (see page 44).

ON THE SIDE

SHEERMAL

This rich and flavoursome bread is a speciality in Lucknow and in Mughal courts all over India. Originally baked in seldom seen iron tandoors in India, this version cooks just as well in an oven. The trick is to incorporate the ghee into the dough slowly, adding little at a time so that the fat is dispersed evenly through the entire dough.

MAKES 16

400ml milk
3 tablespoons caster sugar
1 drop of rose water or screwpine essence (available as kewra water in most good Asian stores)
1½ teaspoons salt
450g plain flour
1 tablespoon melon seeds
½ teaspoon ground cardamom
a pinch of baking powder (optional – if you prefer a bread that rises more)
120g ghee, melted, plus 2 tablespoons for brushing
1 teaspoon poppy seeds
2 pinches of saffron strands, soaked in 1 tablespoon of hot water

Heat the milk in a saucepan until warm, then add the sugar and stir until it dissolves completely. Add the rose or screwpine water and remove from the heat. Allow to cool, then add the salt.

Mix the flour in a mixing bowl with the melon seeds, ground cardamom and baking powder, if using. Add the cooled milk and mix well. Mix into very soft dough, then cover with a damp cloth and set aside for at least 15 minutes.

Remove the cloth and knead the dough again. Add the ghee into the dough, little by little, and incorporate it into the dough using your fingers. Store it in cool place again for 15 minutes to allow it to firm up. Divide the dough equally into 16 pieces. Cover and chill in the fridge for another 10 minutes.

Preheat oven to 180ºC/Gas Mark 4.

Roll out the balls into circles 10cm in diameter and 2.5mm thick. Prick all over with a fork. Arrange them on a greased baking tray, sprinkle with poppy seeds on top and bake in the preheated oven for 10–12 minutes. Remove from the oven, brush with the saffron solution and bake for a further 5–8 minutes.

Serve immediately, brushed with melted ghee.

NAAN BREAD

This popular bread is usually made by slapping a disc of dough onto the side of a charcoal-fired tandoor oven. Now we can reveal a new way of making naan without a tandoor oven.

MAKES 16

37g sugar
1 egg
400ml whole milk
1½ teaspoons baking powder
1 tablespoon salt
750g plain flour
50ml vegetable oil
1 tablespoon nigella seeds

Mix the sugar and egg into the milk. In a separate bowl, mix the baking powder and salt into the flour. Add the milk solution to the flour mix and knead lightly to make soft dough. Take care not to work the gluten too much or the dough becomes too stretchy. When all the ingredients are mixed thoroughly, add the oil and mix lightly. Cover the bowl with a damp cloth and leave to rest for 15 minutes in a warm place.

Preheat your grill to maximum power and keep it ready.

Divide the dough into 16 pieces and roll out each into a circle approximately 5cm in diameter. Sprinkle the nigella seeds over the circles, then roll each circle again until it reaches 10-12cm diameter and 3–4mm thick.

Place a few large, heavy-based frying pans on the hob and, when they're good and hot, place two naan breads in each one and cook for a couple of minutes until they start to colour lightly underneath. Remove the pan from the hob and place directly under the grill for a minute or so, until the bread puffs up and colours a little. Voilà! Your naan bread is ready and you did not even need a tandoor oven!

Tip
You can get as creative as you like with toppings for naan: before baking, try sprinkling them with turmeric, crushed chilli, fresh coriander, garlic, grated cheese, pesto, sun-dried tomatoes, olives – quite simply anything you fancy!

Clockwise from top left: Naan (page 169); Layered Paratha (opposite); Chapati; Stuffed Paratha (pages 30–31); Sheermal (page 168); Triangular Paratha; Southern Indian Layered Paratha

LAYERED PARATHA

These layered parathas are the type traditionally served daily for breakfast, lunch and dinner in south India. This version may take slightly longer to make, but I find it quite therapeutic. Trust me on this!

More and more supermarkets sell ready-made frozen parathas, but when you make your own, you can add different spices, chillies, masalas – whatever you fancy. Try, for example, adding a teaspoon of nigella seeds and a teaspoon of carom seeds. Little beats the satisfaction of having made your own.

MAKES 8

550g plain flour, plus about 50g extra for dusting
1 tablespoon vegetable oil
a pinch of sugar
1 teaspoon salt
2 tablespoons vegetable oil or ghee

Put the flour, oil, sugar and salt in a bowl with 290ml water. Mix together and knead lightly to make a smooth dough. Cover with a damp cloth and leave to rest for 15 minutes.

Divide the dough in 8 equal pieces and roll each into a smooth, round ball. Flatten one ball at a time with the palm of your hand. Sprinkle a little of the reserved flour on the work surface and roll the dough into a circle 15–20cm in diameter.

Brush the top with oil or ghee and sprinkle with a little more flour. Fold the flattened dough into a strip roughly 2.5cm wide, folding the dough like a concertina. Coil the concertina strip loosely to form a layered ball. Drizzle with a little oil or ghee and leave to rest for 10–12 minutes, covered with a damp cloth or clingfilm.

Using a rolling pin, roll out each coil into a circle 12–15cm in diameter and about 5mm thick.

Heat a heavy-based frying pan or flat griddle over a high heat, add one of the rolled coils and cook for 2–3 minutes, until the dough begins to dry out and colours on the bottom. Turn over and cook the dough on the other side, then reduce the heat to medium. Brush the top of the bread with oil or ghee and flip it over again until it is golden and crisp on the outside. You will notice the bread puffs up and the layers should separate as it cooks. The application of ghee between the layers facilitates this, and, as the steam inside the bread builds up, the layers separate. Cook the remaining breads in the same way, wrapping them loosely in foil to keep warm until they are all cooked.

These are excellent with the Duck's Egg Curry (see page 29).

ON THE SIDE

CUMIN-ROASTED POTATOES

Inspired by both the very homely *jeera aloo* found in Indian households and traditional roast spuds from a British household, this recipe combines the best of both worlds. There is something so comforting about home-style potatoes, and everyone has their own favourites.

SERVES 4-6

1kg Maris Piper or King Edward
  potatoes
100g duck fat or 100ml vegetable oil
1 tablespoon whole cumin seeds
1 tablespoon crushed chilli flakes
2 tablespoons chopped coriander
sea salt

Preheat oven to 200ºC/Gas Mark 6. Put a roasting tin (one big enough to take the potatoes in a single layer) in the oven to warm up.

Peel the potatoes and cut into 5cm chunks. Drop the potatoes into a large pan and pour in just enough water to barely cover them. Add sea salt flakes to season, then bring the water to a boil. As soon as the water reaches a full rolling boil, lower the heat and simmer the potatoes uncovered, reasonably vigorously, for 2 minutes.

Meanwhile, put your choice of fat into the hot roasting tin and heat it in the oven for a few minutes, so it's really hot.

Drain the potatoes in a colander and shake the colander back and forth a few times to bruise and fluff up the outsides. Sprinkle with the cumin seeds and chilli flakes, and give another shake or two so they are evenly and thinly coated. Carefully put the potatoes into the hot fat – they will sizzle as they go in – then use a spoon to turn and roll them around so they are coated all over with the fat. Spread them out in a single layer, making sure they have plenty of room.

Place the potatoes in the oven and roast for 15 minutes, then take them out and turn them over. Roast for another 15 minutes and turn them again. Roast for a further 10–15 minutes, or for however long it takes to get them really golden and crisp. The spices will speckle the potatoes. Scatter with more salt and chopped coriander and serve straight away.

MASALA-SAUTÉED POTATOES

Traditionally potatoes will be simply cut into thin strips about 5cm in length and then quickly sautéed in mustard oil with a few fenugreek seeds, perhaps a couple of green chillies and garlic. Here I've added onion rings and serve the potatoes either on their own or as an accompaniment to meats, such as steak.

SERVES 4
(AS A SIDE)

2 tablespoons mustard or vegetable oil
½ teaspoon fenugreek seeds (or cumin seeds)
3 large Desiree or another starchy potatoes, peeled and sliced into discs 3–4mm thick

2 green chillies, chopped
2 garlic cloves, finely grated
½ teaspoon ground turmeric
1 teaspoon salt
1 red onion, sliced into rings
½ bunch coriander, chopped

Heat the oil in a large frying pan. Add the fenugreek or cumin seeds and when they start to crackle, add the potatoes and sauté over a high heat for 3–4 minutes. Add the chillies, garlic, turmeric and salt and sauté for a further 3–4 minutes until the potatoes start to turn golden brown.

Add the onion rings and stir-fry for a couple more minutes until the onions turn caramelised but are still crunchy and the potatoes become crisp. Sprinkle over the coriander and serve immediately.

MAHARASHTRIAN GRATED CARROT SALAD

As the name suggests, this recipe originates from Maharashtra, and it's a simple, quick and easy dish to put together. Speed aside, it's healthy, nutritious and what's best of all, delicious!

SERVES 4
(AS A SIDE)

6 carrots
100g roasted peanuts, half crushed
   and half left whole
1 tablespoon vegetable oil
1½ teaspoons cumin seeds
1 green chilli, chopped
1 teaspoon salt, to taste
a pinch of sugar (optional)
juice of ½ lemon
2 tablespoons chopped coriander

Grate the carrots using the coarse side of a box grater. Tip into a mixing bowl and add the crushed peanuts.

Heat the oil in a small pan, add the cumin seeds and chilli and fry for about a minute until they crackle. Allow to cool, then add to the grated carrots.

Add salt to taste and a pinch of sugar if needed. Add the whole roasted peanuts, squeeze over the lemon juice and garnish with coriander leaves.

BEANS IN TEMPURA BATTER

An ode to Hunan, possibly the best Chinese restaurant in the world. This is my take on a Hunan favourite.

SERVES 6
(AS A SIDE)

500g fine beans, topped and tailed
seasoned flour, for dusting

For the tempura batter
75g plain flour
50g cornflour
1 teaspoon baking powder
½ teaspoon fine sea salt
200–225ml ice-cold sparkling mineral
   water or soda water
5–6 ice cubes

For the garlic and chilli seasoning
2 tablespoons vegetable oil
4 garlic cloves, finely chopped
4 cloves
1 tablespoon crushed chilli flakes
1 teaspoon sugar
1 tablespoon chopped coriander
4 tablespoons soy sauce

For the seasoning, heat the oil in a small frying pan, then add the chopped garlic and cloves until crisp. Remove from the heat, then add the chilli flakes, sugar, coriander and soy sauce. Cool and set aside.

For the tempura batter, mix this just as you are about to cook. Sift the plain flour and cornflour into a large mixing bowl with the baking powder and sea salt. Whisk in the ice-cold sparkling mineral water along with the ice cubes using a whisk, but don't over-beat (a few lumps don't matter). The batter needs to be thick enough to coat your finger. Use immediately.

Sprinkle the beans with seasoned flour and shake off any excess. Dip the beans in the batter and deep fry in hot oil at 190ºC for a minute or two until crisp. Remove and season, pour over the crisp garlic and chilli seasoning and serve immediately.

SUNCHOKE PODIMAS

These are much like the filling you find inside dosa pancakes, but the Jerusalem artichoke gives it a wonderful smokiness and a deep earthy flavour, which I absolutely adore. I hope you like it as much! These make a great topping for Uttapam (see page 33) or even a tasty filling for a quick wrap.

SERVES 6-8

1kg Jerusalem artichokes, unpeeled, but thoroughly washed
1 green chilli, slit lengthways
1 red onion, sliced
2cm piece of ginger, finely chopped
1 teaspoon ground turmeric
salt
2 tablespoons chopped coriander
juice of 1 lemon

For tempering
1 tablespoon vegetable oil
10 fresh curry leaves
1 dried red chilli
1 teaspoon urad dal
1 teaspoon black mustard seeds
a pinch of asafoetida

Bring a pan of salted water to the boil. Add the Jerusalem artichokes and simmer for about 20–25 minutes, until they are tender. Drain well and set aside.

When the artichokes are cool enough to handle, peel them and return them to the pan. Crush them coarsely, then set aside.

For the tempering, heat the oil in a large, heavy-based frying pan to smoking point and add all the tempering ingredients. When the seeds crackle and the curry leaves wilt, add the chilli, red onion, ginger, turmeric and salt and stir on a high heat for 2 minutes. Add the mashed artichokes, mix together and gently reheat. Stir through the coriander and lemon juice and combine well.

CABBAGE PORIAL

This is traditionally served as a vegetable side dish in south India. It makes an excellent accompaniment to meat and fish dishes.

SERVES 4

3 tablespoons vegetable or corn oil
1 teaspoon mustard seeds
2 whole dried red chillies
1 teaspoon chana dal (split yellow chickpeas)
10 curry leaves
2 onions, chopped
1cm piece of ginger, chopped
3 green chillies, finely chopped
1 teaspoon ground turmeric
250g white cabbage, shredded
2 teaspoons salt
50g grated fresh coconut

Heat the oil in a wok over a high heat. Add the mustard seeds and when they start to crackle, add the red chillies and chana dal and fry for a minute until the chillies darken in colour.

Add the curry leaves and the onions and sauté until the onions become translucent. Add the chopped ginger, green chilli and turmeric and stir-fry for a minute. Add the shredded cabbage and the salt and cook for 3–4 minutes, stirring constantly. If the cabbage is not cooked completely, sprinkle with a little water, reduce the heat, cover with a lid and cook for another 2–3 minutes. Add the grated coconut and sauté for a minute, then serve hot as an accompaniment.

CHICKPEA CURRY

This is a recipe for traditional Punjabi-style chickpeas, but you can easily add diced chorizo to it while adding chickpeas and water for a smoky rich meaty chana masala. This dish works well on its own, served simply with a flatbread of your choice, or serve as an accompaniment to a roasted piece of fish.

SERVES 4

3 red onions, roughly chopped
1cm piece of ginger, roughly chopped
3 garlic cloves
1 green chili
1 tablespoon vegetable oil
1–2 small pieces of cinnamon
6 peppercorns
1–2 green cardamom pods
1 bay leaf
2 tomatoes, diced
1 teaspoon caster sugar
1½ teaspoons salt
1 tablespoon ground cumin
1 tablespoon ground coriander
½ teaspoon ground turmeric
400g can of chickpeas, drained and
    rinsed
100g cooking chorizo, diced almost
    the same size as chickpeas
    (optional)
1 tablespoon Chana Masala
    (see page 224; alternatively use
    Garam Masala, see page 225)
juice of ½ lemon
2 tablespoons chopped coriander

Blend the onions, garlic, ginger and chilli to a coarse paste in a food processor with 2–3 tablespoons of water.

Heat the oil in a deep, wide, heavy-based pan over a medium heat. Fry the bay leaf, cinnamon, peppercorns and cardamoms for 1 minute. Add the onion mixture and the tomatoes and sauté for 8–10 minutes until the mixture starts changing color and becomes darker.

Add the sugar, salt, cumin, ground coriander and turmeric. Cook for another few minutes, mixing well. Add the chickpeas, chorizo and 450ml water. Bring to a boil, then reduce the heat, cover with a lid and simmer over a low heat for 20–30 minutes. Check to see that there is enough liquid in the pan, adding small quantities of water if it starts drying up.

Stir in the garam masala and finish with the lemon juice and chopped coriander.

Clockwise from top-left: Green Moong Lentil Tadka (page 187); Rajasthani Five-Lentil Mix (page 184); White Urad Lentils with Cloves (page 185); Chickpea Curry (page 181); Sambhar (page 186)

ON THE SIDE

RAJASTHANI FIVE-LENTIL MIX

Panchmael means mix of five and hence the name of this dish, *Panchmael dal*. A mixed lentil dish can be made up of as many as five different types, but the three easily available in larger supermarkets and health food stores are red, moong and chana. A visit to an Asian grocery store is worth the excursion for the others, but it's not essential. You can even make the dish with any one type – just increase the quantity accordingly.

SERVES 4

2 tablespoons split green moong lentils
2 tablespoons toor dal (yellow gram)
2 tablespoons split chana dal
2 tablespoons split white urad lentils
2 tablespoons red split lentils
½ teaspoon ground turmeric
1½ teaspoons salt
2 tablespoons ghee
1 large onion, finely chopped
½ teaspoon red chilli powder
1 teaspoon garam masala
1 tomato, chopped
1 tablespoon chopped coriander
juice of ½ lemon

For the tadka
1 tablespoon ghee
1 whole dried red chilli
½ teaspoon whole cumin seeds
4 cloves
2 garlic cloves, finely chopped

First boil the lentils. Mix them together in a sieve, wash under cold running water, then let them soak in a bowl of cold water for 20 minutes. Drain and tip into a saucepan, add 600ml water, half the turmeric and 1 teaspoon of salt and bring to the boil. Skim off the white froth whenever necessary, then cover, reduce the heat and simmer over a low heat. Cook the lentils, except for the chana dal, until all are well mashed. This should take 20–25 minutes.

Heat the ghee in a frying pan and when hot, add the onion. Cook for about 10 minutes until it turns golden brown, then add the remaining turmeric and salt, chilli powder and garam masala and sauté for a minute, then add the tomato and cook for 2–3 minutes until soft. Pour this mixture over the lentils, and bring the broth to boil. If the lentils begin to thicken, add some boiling water and keep stirring to ensure they don't stick to the bottom of the pan. Finish with fresh coriander and a squeeze of lemon. Keep the lentils warm.

For the tadka, heat the ghee in a small frying pan until it reaches smoking point. Add the whole red chilli, cumin seeds, cloves and garlic in that order and in quick succession. As the spices begin to crackle and pop and the garlic begins to turn golden, pour the contents of the frying pan over the dal and cover the pan with a lid. Leave covered for 2 minutes to let the lentils absorb the flavours. Remove the lid, stir and serve immediately.

WHITE URAD LENTILS WITH CLOVES

These white urad lentils are quite different from our everyday lentils. They have more texture and are quite crunchy compared to most other variations that break down and become quite brothy. Also, the use of cloves in the tempering is rather unusual. This is the kind of lentil dish to serve with chapattis, poories or a bread of some description, rather than with rice.

SERVES 4-6
(AS A SIDE)

100g urad dal or split black urad
2 tablespoons vegetable oil
3 cloves
2 bay leaves
1 teaspoon cumin seeds
2.5cm piece of ginger, finely chopped
1 onion, sliced
2 green chillies, chopped
1 tomato, diced
½ teaspoon ground turmeric red chilli powder, to taste
1 teaspoon salt 1 teaspoon lemon juice
a pinch of garam masala
1 tablespoon finely chopped coriander

Wash the dal in two or three changes of water, then soak in a bowl of water for 10–15 minutes.

Bring the dal to the boil in a pan of 1.2 litres of cold water, then simmer, covered, and boil for 20–25 minutes until the lentils are just cooked but not disintegrated. Drain and reserve the lentils.

Heat the oil in a frying pan and add cloves, bay leaves and cumin seeds. When they start crackling and popping, add the ginger, onion and green chillies and stir-fry for about 10 minutes until golden brown. Add the tomato and fry until it softens, then add the turmeric, chilli powder and salt and fry for a minute or so. Add the drained dal and lemon juice and mix very gently to avoid breaking up the lentils.

Sprinkle with garam masala and garnish with coriander. Serve hot.

SAMBHAR

This broth makes a hot, slightly sour accompaniment to the otherwise dry and slightly plain dosa- and uttapam-based breakfast dishes. It has the consistency of a medium-thick soup and can also be just served on its own with simple, plain boiled rice.

SERVES 6-8
(AS A SIDE)

150g toor dal
½ teaspoon ground turmeric
2 teaspoons salt
1 tablespoon vegetable or corn oil
a sprig of fresh curry leaves
1 white onion, thinly sliced
10 small shallots, each roughly
    chopped into 2–3 pieces
50g green beans, cut into 2.5cm
    lengths
2 carrots, cut into 2.5cm chunks
2 baby aubergines, quartered (or 1
    standard-sized aubergine)
2 tablespoons Sambhar Masala (see
    recipe below)
3 tablespoons tamarind paste
½ teaspoon red chilli powder
1 teaspoon sugar

For tempering
1 tablespoon vegetable or corn oil
1½ teaspoons mustard seeds
1 dried red chilli
¼ teaspoon asafoetida
a sprig of curry leaves

For the Sambhar Masala
1 teaspoon coriander seeds
2 teaspoons cumin seeds
1 tablespoon chana dal
6 dried red chillies
1½ teaspoons black peppercorns
2 tablespoons grated coconut
½ teaspoon fenugreek seeds
a sprig of curry leaves

Wash the lentils in cold running water, then leave to soak for 15 minutes. Drain well and place in a heavy-based pan with 800ml cold water. Bring to the boil, skim off any scum from the surface, then add the turmeric and half the salt and simmer for 30 minutes.

Meanwhile, heat the oil in a separate pan. Add the curry leaves and onion and sauté for about 10 minutes until the onion is soft. Add the shallots, green beans, carrots and aubergines and sauté for 5 minutes. Now add the Sambar Masala, tamarind paste and chilli powder and cook for another 5 minutes. Add this mixture to the lentils when they have finished their simmering. Stir well, adding a little water if the mixture is too thick. Simmer until the vegetables are soft, and then add the sugar and the remaining salt.

To temper the mixture, heat the oil in a small pan and add the mustard seeds. When they crackle, add the dried chilli, asafoetida and curry leaves, give them a stir and pour the mixture over the broth. Mix well and serve.

For the Sambhar Masala
Dry roast all the ingredients in a frying pan, cool, then grind to a powder in a spice grinder. Store in an airtight container and use within two weeks.

GREEN MOONG LENTIL TADKA

In Punjab and the rest of northern India, the term *tadka* refers to tempering cumin, chillies, onions, etc before using them to finish lentils and similar dishes. The final addition of spices cooked in hot ghee gives them their smokiness and a pronounced kick. In roadside cafés along the highways of eastern India the meaning has become distorted, and *tadka* now refers to a dish of green moong lentils. I've seen many variations of this lentil dish, some with a sauce made from chicken, lamb or even egg. This is the lentil version.

SERVES 8-10 (AS A SIDE)

120g whole green moong lentils
1½ teaspoons salt
1 tablespoon ginger paste (see page 226)
2 bay leaves
3 black cardamom pods
2 tablespoons vegetable or corn oil
1 teaspoon cumin seeds
4 garlic cloves, chopped
2 onions, very finely chopped
1½ teaspoons red chilli powder
1 tablespoon ground coriander
2 very ripe tomatoes, puréed
2 green chillies, finely chopped
½ teaspoon garam masala
15g butter
juice of ½ lemon
chopped coriander, to garnish

Wash the lentils, then leave them to soak in cold water for 20 minutes. Drain the lentils and place in a pan with 1.2 litres of water, salt, ginger paste, bay leaves and black cardamom pods. Bring to the boil, cover with a lid and simmer for 30–40 minutes until the lentils are soft but still hold their shape. Turn the heat off but do not drain.

Heat the oil in a large, heavy-based pan and add the cumin seeds. When they crackle, add the garlic and fry for 1–2 minutes until golden. Add the onions and cook over a high heat for 6–8 minutes until golden brown, then stir in the chilli powder and ground coriander. Cook for 3–5 minutes, until the oil starts to separate from the mixture around the edge of the pan. Add the puréed tomatoes and cook for 6–8 minutes.

Pour the lentils and their cooking water into this mixture, bring to the boil and simmer for 10–12 minutes. Add the green chillies and garam masala and cook gently until the onion mix and lentils are thoroughly combined and the lentils thicken the mixture slightly. Simmer for 2–3 minutes, then add the butter and lemon juice. Transfer to a serving bowl.

Serve hot, garnished with fresh coriander and accompanied by layered parathas (see page 171) or naan bread (see page 169).

Tip
If you wish, you could stretch any leftover chicken or lamb curry by adding plain boiled green moong lentils to it and heating through thoroughly.

ON THE SIDE

From left to right: 'Gunpowder' (page 192); Pumpkin Seed Chutney (page 193); Green Coriander Chutney (page 190); Green Coconut Chutney (page 190); Tomato and Coconut Chutney (page 191); Plum Chutney (page 128); Bramley Apple Chutney (page 195); Mock Wasabi (page 193); Nepalese Sesame and Peanut Chutney (page 191)

ON THE SIDE

GREEN COCONUT CHUTNEY

This is simple yet versatile chutney to accompany any south Indian dish. The mint leaves are my own little addition.

MAKES ABOUT 400G

2 tablespoons chana dal (split yellow Bengal gram)
grated white flesh of 1 coconut
1 large bunch (approximately 50g) coriander leaves
1 bunch (approximately 25g) mint leaves
5 green chillies, chopped
1 teaspoon salt
vegetable oil or water, to blend into a paste

For tempering
1 tablespoon vegetable oil
10 fresh curry leaves
¼ teaspoon black mustard seeds

Dry roast the chana dal in a frying pan over a medium heat for 2–3 minutes.

Put the chana dal, coconut, coriander, mint, chillies and salt in a blender or food processor and blend to a soft, spoonable consistency. Add a couple of tablespoons of vegetable oil and/or water to help the chutney blend. It's not important to get a smooth, fine paste – a coarse texture is fine for this chutney.

To temper the chutney, heat the oil to smoking point and add the curry leaves and mustard seeds. As soon as they start to crackle, add to the chutney and stir through, then remove the pan from the heat.

This chutney can be stored in a refrigerator for up to 3 days but it is best eaten on the day it is made.

GREEN CORIANDER CHUTNEY

This is probably the most versatile chutney of them all – fresh, zingy, sharp, it works well with kebabs as well as a filling in wraps. Added to thinned yoghurt it makes for a vibrant green, fresh raita too.

MAKES 300G

200g coriander leaves and stalks, washed thoroughly to remove any grit
40g mint leaves (optional)
6 garlic cloves, peeled
6 Thai green chillies, stalks removed
6 tablespoons vegetable oil
2 teaspoons salt
1 teaspoon sugar
juice of 1 lemon

Blend together the herbs, garlic, and chillies until a soft, spoonable consistency. Cover with the oil and store in the fridge until required.

To use, mix with the salt, sugar and lemon juice, check the seasoning and use as needed.

This chutney will keep in the fridge for 2–3 days, but once the salt and lemon have been added, it is best used straight away.

TOMATO AND COCONUT CHUTNEY

This is an example of a twice-cooked chutney from southern India. It is cooked once before blending and again briefly with the hot oil and spices. It can be stored in a fridge for 3 days, but it's best enjoyed fresh.

MAKES ABOUT 300G

1 tablespoon vegetable oil
10 fresh curry leaves
½ teaspoon fennel seeds
1 onion, chopped
3 tomatoes, chopped
1½ teaspoons red chilli powder
grated white flesh of 1 coconut
30g roasted chana dal (split yellow chickpeas, sold as daria dal in Asian stores)
1 teaspoon salt

For tempering
2 tablespoons vegetable oil
5–10 fresh curry leaves
1 dried red chilli
1 teaspoon black mustard seeds

Heat the oil in a large heavy-based pan and add the curry leaves and fennel seeds. When the seeds crackle, add the onion and sauté over a medium heat for 10 minutes until golden. Add the tomatoes and chilli powder and cook for 5–8 minutes, stirring occasionally, until the tomatoes have softened. Stir in the coconut and cook for another 10 minutes until all the liquid has evaporated.

Remove the pan from the heat and leave the chutney to cool. In a food processor blend the chutney with the roasted chana dal and a little water. Mix in the salt. To temper the chutney, heat the oil to smoking point. Add the curry leaves, red chilli and mustard seeds. When the seeds crackle, pour over the chutney and stir through.

NEPALESE SESAME AND PEANUT CHUTNEY

This chutney is often referred to as gorkha chutney, probably named after the Nepalese folk, or also as momo chutney in restaurants as it is often served with steamed pork dumplings or vegetarian momos.

MAKES 400G

1 tablespoon vegetable oil
1 whole dried red chilli
¼ teaspoon fenugreek seeds
2.5cm piece of fresh ginger, cut into strips
2–3 garlic cloves, peeled
2 green chillies, slit
125g white sesame seeds
1 red onion, sliced
¼ teaspoon ground turmeric
½ teaspoon red chilli powder
1 teaspoon ground coriander
½ teaspoon ground cumin
125g peanuts, roasted and ground
2 tomatoes, chopped
½ teaspoon salt
a pinch of sugar
a pinch of garam masala
juice of ½ lemon

Heat the oil in a saucepan, add the red chillies and fenugreek and stir until they release their flavours. Add the ginger, garlic, green chillies and sesame seeds and sauté for a minute. Add the onion and stir until it becomes translucent. Add the powdered spices and stir for a minute. Add the peanuts, followed by the tomatoes, salt and sugar and cook for 3–4 minutes until the tomatoes are soft and tender. Sprinkle in the garam masala and take the saucepan off the heat. Blend to a smooth paste and stir in the lemon juice. Refrigerate until you use and serve with momos or as a dip. The chutney will keep for 3 days in a fridge.

ON THE SIDE

SPROUTED MOONG CHUTNEY

Inspired from the ever-popular hummus, this is slightly different as it uses sprouted moong, rather than cooked chickpeas, as a base. There is a freshness and texture as a result, and it tastes great.

MAKES 450G

350g sprouted moong beans
1 teaspoon Chaat Masala (see page 224)
2–3 garlic cloves, peeled
1 tablespoon tahini paste
1½ tablespoons sugar
½ teaspoon salt
50ml olive oil
juice of 1 lemon

Mix all ingredients together, then blend to a fine purée. Refrigerate until use.

This keeps for 3–4 days in the fridge. You can also serve it as a dip with bread.

DRY LENTIL CHUTNEY

Otherwise known as 'Gunpowder', this chutney is originally from Karnataka in south-west India. We serve this with asparagus accompanied by Curried Yoghurt (see page 225).

MAKES 220G

100g chana dal
100g urad dal, washed
1 teaspoon sesame seeds (optional)
3 whole dried red chillies
½ teaspoon asafoetida
1½ teaspoons peppercorns
10–15 curry leaves, dried or fresh
½ teaspoon salt
2 tablespoons ghee (optional)

Dry roast the lentils in a dry frying pan over a medium-high heat for 2–3 minutes. Halfway through, just as the lentils are beginning to change colour, add the sesame seeds, if using. Continue to lightly roast, stirring quickly, until the lentils give off a nutty aroma. In a separate pan, dry roast the chillies for 2–3 minutes.

Alternatively, you can preheat the oven to 170–180ºC/Gas Mark 3–4 and roast the lentils for 6–10 minutes until nutty and slightly coloured (add the sesame seeds halfway through, if using). You may need to move the lentils around for even roasting.

Allow to cool, then grind them to a coarse powder with the spices and salt and store in an airtight container. The mixture will keep for 2–3 weeks.

To serve, if you wish, mix the powder with a little melted ghee or clarified butter to turn it into a wet chutney.

PUMPKIN SEED CHUTNEY

MOCK WASABI CHUTNEY

Originally inspired by the cooking of a friend's mother, this recipe originates in Nainital, in the northern state of Uttarakhand. The roasting of tomatoes and garlic adds a depth of flavour but still retains freshness.

MAKES 350G

2 tomatoes
2 garlic cloves, unpeeled
225g pumpkin seeds
5cm piece of fresh ginger, peeled and chopped
4 green chillies
½ bunch fresh coriander leaves
3 tablespoons vegetable oil
1 teaspoon salt
½ teaspoon sugar
juice of 1 lemon

Preheat oven to 220ºC/Gas Mark 7.

Place the tomatoes and garlic cloves in a baking dish and roast for 20 minutes. Allow to cool.

Dry-roast the pumpkin seeds in a frying pan for 2–3 minutes until aromatic. Allow to cool, then grind coarsely.

Peel the skin from the roasted tomatoes and garlic. Mix with the rest of the ingredients and blend to a smooth paste using a blender or food processor. Refrigerate until use.

Wasabi-like to look at, wasabi-like to taste, but it isn't quite that! Give it a go and get your friends and guests to guess what it's made from. This green pea relish makes for an excellent accompaniment to grilled or steamed fish and seafood dishes.

MAKES 350G

300g fresh green peas (shelled weight)
1cm piece of ginger, peeled
3 garlic cloves
2 green chillies
½ teaspoon salt
½ teaspoon sugar
2 tablespoons mustard oil
juice of ½ lime
½ teaspoon nigella seeds

Place the green peas in a blender with the ginger, garlic, green chillies, salt, sugar and mustard oil and blend to a fine purée. Check the seasoning and stir through lime juice. Sprinkle the nigella seeds over the top and serve.

ON THE SIDE

QUINCE CHUTNEY

This is a great chutney to serve with grilled game, as a dip for breads or as an accompaniment to cheese.

MAKES 800G

5 quince
juice of 1 lemon
100ml white wine vinegar
1 teaspoon black onion seeds
2 whole dried red chillies
2 bay leaves
400g sugar

Peel and cut each quince into 1cm dice, keeping the dice in a bowl of water and lemon juice until ready to cook.

Drain the quince, then mix with all the remaining ingredients. Cook in a heavy-based pan until it comes to a boil, then reduce the heat and simmer for about 40 minutes until the syrup thickens and the colour changes to become almost purple.

Remove from the heat, cool and refrigerate until use.

If you wish, spoon into sterilized jars and used within 2–3 months.

PINEAPPLE DIPPING SAUCE

An excellent fresh accompaniment to salads as a dressing or a dip. Also serve it with grilled or fried snacks, such as barbecued chicken or spring rolls.

MAKES 250G

250g fresh pineapple, some finely chopped and some crushed to a rough salsa, using the flat side of a large knife
2 tablespoons fish sauce
1 tablespoon chopped coriander
1 red chilli, finely chopped
juice of 1 lemon

Mix all the ingredients together. If the mixture is too thick, add a few tablespoons of pineapple juice. Chill in the fridge until ready to use. The sauce will keep for a couple of days in the fridge but is best enjoyed fresh.

BRAMLEY APPLE CHUTNEY

I like to serve this chutney with scallops, but it is also good spread over biscuits and served with cheese. If you don't have Bramley apples, use any other cooking apple.

MAKES ABOUT 750G

4 Bramley apples (750–800g), peeled, cored and chopped into 1cm dice
150ml white wine vinegar
4 green cardamom pods
1 teaspoon fennel seeds
1 bay leaf
½ teaspoon salt
100g sugar

Place all the ingredients in a saucepan and bring to the boil. Reduce the heat to medium and cook for about 15 minutes until the syrup thickens and the apple turns soft and glossy. Stir the pan from time to time to prevent the chutney catching on the base of the pan.

Cool the chutney and serve as an accompaniment.
It will keep in an airtight jar in the fridge for 2–3 weeks

MUSTARD AIOLI

This is great with Amritsar-Spiced Fish Fingers (see page 142), but would also work well with the Potato Bonda Burgers (see page 57) or one of the salads featured in this book.

MAKES 160ML

120ml mayonnaise (homemade or bought)
1 heaped tablespoon Dijon mustard
1 heaped tablespoon wholegrain mustard
1 teaspoon honey
2 garlic cloves, crushed to a paste
a pinch of caster sugar
sea salt and freshly ground black pepper

Whisk the mayonnaise, Dijon mustard, wholegrain mustard, honey and garlic together, then sprinkle with sugar, salt and pepper, stirring to mix. Cover the bowl and refrigerate for a couple of hours.

ENDING ON A SWEET NOTE

TOFFEE BANANAS

This is probably the first dessert I ordered in a restaurant – I loved it so much that I still remember it! However, very few Chinese restaurants still feature this on their menus, but the one place where you find toffee banana as a regular feature is my own kitchen at home.

SERVES 4

50g self-raising flour
25g cornflour, plus extra for dusting
a pinch of ground ginger
100–120ml cold water, enough to get a smooth coating batter
1 teaspoon vegetable oil
oil, for deep-frying
2–3 bananas, sliced 2.5cm thick
150g sugar
½ teaspoon each black and white sesame seeds, for sprinkling

To make the batter, whisk together the self-raising flour, cornflour and ground ginger in a bowl, then add the water and mix well until smooth. Stir in the teaspoon of vegetable oil.

Toss the banana slices in the extra cornflour to coat lightly. Using a skewer, dip each banana slice in the batter.

Heat the oil in a deep pan or deep fat fryer to 170–180ºC. Cook the bananas in batches for about 4 minutes until golden and crisp. Drain on kitchen paper.

To make the caramel coating, place the sugar in a large, heavy-based frying pan over a medium heat and cook, shaking the pan occasionally, until a caramel forms. Remove from the heat, sprinkle over the sesame seeds, then working quickly and one at a time, add the fried banana to the caramel and turn to coat. Drop the caramel-coated bananas into a large bowl of iced water, one piece at a time, to set the caramel. Drain immediately. Leave to cool for a few minutes before serving with ice cream.

BEBINCA

The traditional Goan dessert is a favourite. The process of making a cake out of several layers of cooked pancake may appear tedious but once you get the hang of it, it's really quite simple.

SERVES 8

400g sugar
125g plain flour
500ml coconut milk
6 egg yolks
a pinch of salt
8 green cardamom pods, ground
50g ghee
1 tablespoon almond flakes, toasted, or toasted desiccated coconut, to garnish

Place the sugar in a pan with 200ml water and bring to the boil. Boil until the sugar dissolves and bubbles. Turn the heat down and keep the mixture simmering. Dip a spatula in the syrup, lift it out and touch it with the tip of your forefinger to pick a drop of syrup. Be very careful as it can burn your finger! Touch your forefinger with your thumb and pull apart slowly, to see how many threads are stretched between your finger and thumb – you want it to reach one-thread consistency, ie the mixture stretches in a single thread. Turn off the heat off as soon as it reaches this stage. If using a sugar thermometer, single thread syrup is approximately 104–105ºC. Cool to lukewarm.

Mix the flour with the coconut milk until smooth, add the sugar syrup and mix well. Beat the egg yolks just enough to mix them together, then add to the flour mixture. Add the salt and ground cardamom. You want a thin, flowing batter that will spread thinly in the pan, so add a little water at this stage if your batter is too thick. The thinner the layers of pancake, the quicker they will colour under the grill and the more layers you will get on your cake.

Preheat the grill to medium hot.

Heat 1 tablespoon of the ghee in a large non-stick frying pan with a heatproof handle and pour in just enough batter to cover the pan to make a thin pancake. Cook over a low heat until set but not browned. Brush the top of the pancake with some ghee and flash under the grill until it becomes light brown on top.

Pour a second similar quantity of batter on top of the pancake, swirl it to coat evenly and flash under the grill until light brown on top. Repeat the layers of ghee and batter until all the batter is used up.

Cool the pancakes until lukewarm. Turn the pan upside down to remove the bebinca. Slice the pancakes and serve garnished with almond flakes or toasted desiccated coconut.

Serve with an ice cream of your choice. Alternatively, cut into very small pieces and serve as petits fours at the end of the meal.

ENDING ON A SWEET NOTE

MANGO CAKE

This is my favourite cake of all time, and over the years our pastry chef at The Cinnamon Club, Mor Singh Jakhi, has turned this into our favourite cake in the restaurant too. Two medium-sized mangoes (ideally Alphonso) should provide enough fruit for the purée, slices and garnish.

SERVES 6

500ml double cream
70g sugar
200g ripe mango, cut into 1cm cubes
150g ripe mango, thinly sliced for the garnish

For the mango sponge
3 eggs
150g caster sugar
150g plain flour
1 vanilla pod
50g mango purée

For the sugar syrup
200ml warm water
100g sugar

Preheat oven to 170ºC/Gas Mark 3 ½. Line a round 25cm cake tin.

Weigh the three eggs. The caster sugar and flour need to match the weight of the eggs, so you may need to adjust their quantities up or down a little. To make the sponge, first beat the eggs and sugar together until light and at ribbon stage (ie the mixture hangs down from the beaters in ribbons). Fold in the flour. Scrape the seeds out of the vanilla pod and mix with the mango purée. Add this to the mixture and fold in gently. Pour the mixture into the cake tin. Bake in the preheated oven for 30–35 minutes or until a skewer inserted into the centre of the cake comes out clean.

Allow the cake to cool for a couple of minutes, then transfer to a wire rack to cool completely. When cool, refrigerate until ready to serve. To make the sugar syrup, dissolve the sugar and water in a pan, bring to boil, then simmer for 4–5 minutes. Allow to cool before using.

To finish the cake, carefully slice the mango sponge into three layers of equal thickness. Whip the cream with the sugar until it forms medium peaks. Sprinkle about a third of the sugar syrup on the base layer of the sponge, then spread on 100g of cream and half the mango cubes. Place the second layer on top and repeat the same process. Place the third layer on top and sprinkle over the remaining sugar syrup. Cover the cake with the remaining cream and garnish with the mango slices.

LASSI PANNA COTTA

Anyone who has travelled to India in the summer will be familiar with the lassi stalls that pop up all over small towns and cities serving these cooling smoothie-style drinks. I love using the inspiration of lassi as the basis for a simple dessert which is great both for summer afternoons and for entertaining big numbers.

SERVES 6

5 gelatine leaves (10g in total)
500ml full-fat Greek yoghurt
300ml whole milk
125g caster sugar
¼ teaspoon salt
1 teaspoon green cardamom powder
3–4 ripe mangoes, peeled, stoned and flesh chopped into 2.5cm dice
sprinkle of Chaat Masala (see page 224) (optional)

Soak the gelatine leaves in 100ml of cold water to soften them.

In a mixing bowl whisk the yoghurt, milk, sugar, salt and cardamom powder until it turns frothy.

Melt the gelatine in 100ml warm water, then add to the yoghurt mixture. Mix well and pour into individual moulds or serving bowls. Chill in the fridge for a couple of hours, or even overnight if you have the time.

Mix the diced mango (or seasonal fruits) with chaat masala (if using), and set aside for 15 minutes to make a fruit chat. Serve the panna cottas with a mango chat garnish or with any seasonal fruit salad.

SWEET SEMOLINA HALWA

A childhood favourite of mine, *Sooji Ka Halwa* is easy to make and so delicious!

SERVES 4

120ml whole milk
700ml hot water
75g sugar
5 green cardamom pods, split open
75g ghee or clarified butter
200g coarse semolina
50g cashew nuts, coarsely chopped
2 tablespoons raisins or sultanas

Place the milk, water, sugar and cardamom in a large pan and bring to the boil over a medium heat, stirring frequently until the sugar has dissolved. Reduce the heat and simmer for 5–10 minutes or for as long as it takes to roast the semolina in the other pan.

Heat a deep pan over a medium heat. When hot, add the ghee. When it has melted, add the semolina and roast, stirring frequently, until it begins to turn golden and gives off a roasted aroma. The roasted semolina will have the consistency of wet sand. Add the cashews and raisins to the semolina and mix well.

When the semolina is roasted, gently add the milk mixture over a low heat, stirring constantly to prevent lumps forming. If any do form, break them down using the back of the spoon so you get a smooth, paste-like consistency. Cook the mixture for a few minutes until it is thick and begins to come away from the sides of the pan. Turn off the heat and allow the mixture to cool to a warm temperature. Serve in individual bowls.

Alternatively, you could let the mix cool down, then use as a filling for spring rolls, wrapping the halwa in spring roll pastry and frying until crisp, then serving with an ice cream of your choice. See Carrot Halwa Spring Rolls on page 208 for rolling instructions.

COCONUT JAGGERY SOFT ROLL

I first had these rolls in Cochin around 10 years ago, when Rakesh Nair, our head chef at The Cinnamon Club, and I took some journalists to see the spice plantations. These were served to us during one of the home-stays as a mid-morning snack. The flavours, intense sweetness and fresh ingredients and spices left an unforgettable memory. The pancakes are easy enough to make but if not, you can easily substitute them with rice paper rolls (available in good Asian stores) and roll them like Vietnamese summer rolls.

SERVES 4

For the filling
250g grated fresh or frozen coconut
30g desiccated coconut
1 tablespoon raisins
150ml evaporated milk
60g jaggery, grated
3 green cardamom pods, ground
1 tablespoon ground pistachios

For the crêpes
2 tablespoons sugar
65g plain flour
a scant pinch of salt
1 large egg
125ml whole milk
50ml warm water
1 tablespoon melted butter, lukewarm

To serve
sweetened coconut milk (optional)

Mix all the filling ingredients together in a mixing bowl and leave aside for 20 minutes in a warm place.

To make the crêpe batter, whisk together the sugar, flour, salt, egg and milk in a large bowl until well incorporated. Whisk in the warm water. Add the melted butter and whisk again. Strain the batter through a sieve into a clean bowl, then repeat the sieving twice more to make it really smooth and lump free.

Heat a non-stick pan over a medium-high heat. When the pan is hot, spray with just a little oil or wipe the pan with a piece of oiled kitchen paper, then pour in a small ladleful of batter. Tilt the pan and rotate, to make the batter to cover the base of the pan (do this speedily as the batter cooks quickly). Cook for 1 minute over medium-high heat until the underside is lightly browned, then turn the crêpe over and cook for 30 seconds.

Stack the crêpes on a plate and keep warm in a warm oven until they are all cooked. The mixture makes 8–10 crêpes.

Divide the filling into as many parts as the number of crêpes you have made. Shape the filling mix into cylinder and place on the crêpe and fold the crêpes into cylinders. Serve with sweetened coconut milk or simply cut into small pieces.

ENDING ON A SWEET NOTE

CARROT HALWA SPRING ROLLS

Carrot halwa in its traditional form must be India's most recognisable dessert as it is cooked in most Indian homes in winter. My mother makes a mean halwa too, and as much as I loved gorging on bowl after bowlful as a child, I know I can't eat like that any more. In fact, I don't even enjoy it as much, with fatigue setting in as spoon after spoon of the same rich taste, texture and flavour gets the better of my greed!

SERVES 6

60g ghee or clarified butter
250g regular carrots, peeled and
  grated
250g black heritage carrots, peeled
  and grated
100g sugar
2 tablespoons raisins
3 green cardamom pods, ground
250ml evaporated milk
6 sheets of spring roll pastry
  (or filo pastry sheets)
30g butter, melted, for brushing
vegetable oil, for frying

Divide the ghee between two separate pans and heat it up. Add the two different grated carrots to separate pans and sauté for 10 minutes over a low heat until the juices from the carrots evaporate. Add half the sugar, raisins and ground cardamom to each pan and cook until the sugar melts. Divide the evaporated milk between the pans and and cook until each mixture takes on the look of orange-coloured fudge. Spread the mixtures on two trays and let them cool. Divide each mixture into six equal parts.

Take a spring roll pastry sheet and brush the edges with melted butter. Place on a diagonal on a work surface. Place one heap of orange carrot fudge and one heap of black carrot fudge towards the corner closest to you. Take the same corner of the pastry, fold it over the carrot and continue rolling it until you reach almost to the middle of the strip. Tuck in from both sides, then continue rolling until you reach the end of the pastry. Seal the edges with a drop of water. Repeat the same process with the remaining sheets.

Heat a deep pan of oil to 160ºC and deep-fry the spring rolls for 4–5 minutes until they are golden brown. Drain on kitchen paper.

Serve hot with an ice cream of your choice. You could also make these smaller, and serve them as pass around desserts at the end of a canapé meal.

ENDING ON A SWEET NOTE

MALPUA

This recipe is copyright Mrs Singh senior! It is a very simple dessert but a firm family favourite in the Singh household when we were growing up. It is a classic north Indian home recipe that has a million variations and each family believes theirs is the best.

SERVES 4-6

250g plain flour
200g sugar
enough milk to make a smooth
   pouring batter (about 500ml)
½ teaspoon green cardamom powder
2 tablespoons golden raisins
½ banana, mashed (optional)
vegetable oil, for deep frying

Mix together all the ingredients to make a smooth batter, then set aside in the fridge for 2–3 hours to allow the flavours to develop.

Pour the oil into a wok to a depth of around 5cm, then heat to medium-hot.

Mix the batter using a spoon, then pour a spoonful of the batter into oil to deep-fry for 3–4 minutes until the edges are crisp and the middle of the pancakes are still soft. Turn over halfway during the cooking process when the underside is golden and crisp.

Drain using a slotted spoon, let cool for a minute or so, then serve with ice cream of your choice or on its own. This mixture will make approximately 20 pancakes.

MISHTI DOI

Most Bengalis will swear by their own recipe for *mishti doi*. This is a dish that goes beyond being just a dessert, it has transcended to the level of a religion in Kolkata! Here I have tried my best to get the balance between the rich creaminess and fragrance of *mishti doi*, and the freshness and acidity associated with yoghurt.

SERVES 6

1.4 litres whole milk
250g sugar
4 green cardamom pods
4 tablespoons plain live yoghurt, whisked

Preheat oven to 80°C/Gas Mark ¼ and switch off the oven.

Bring the milk to the boil in a heavy-based pan, then reduce the heat. Add two-thirds of the sugar and the cardamom pods to the hot milk. Bring back to the boil, then simmer to reduce to half the quantity.

In the meantime, heat the remaining sugar in a pan over a low heat until the sugar is caramelised. Turn off the heat. Add 2 tablespoons of water to the sugar and stir with a spoon.

Add the caramelised sugar mixture to the milk and stir well. Let the milk cool down until it is just above body temperature (but not hot, around 37–40°C). Then add the yoghurt and stir to mix well. Remove the cardamom pods and discard.

Pour the mixture into four earthenware serving dishes, cover with foil and set for 2–3 hours or overnight in the warm oven. Once the yoghurt is firm, chill it in the fridge for a few hours before serving.

Serve with blueberries, strawberries or a fruit of your choice.

SPICED SCONES

The most popular scone recipe in our household comes from James Martin and this is my adaptation of it. Under much duress, I sometimes add some ginger and cinnamon to it, but to be perfectly honest, the recipe below is just as good without the spice. The other variation I like a lot has fennel seeds and carom seeds instead of the ginger and cinnamon, which gives a slightly savoury result.

MAKES 16

450g strong plain flour, plus extra for dusting
5 teaspoons baking powder
a pinch of salt
2 teaspoons ground cinnamon (optional, or replace with carom seeds)
75g unsalted butter, plus extra for greasing
75g caster sugar (reduce to 40g if making savoury scones)
100g sultanas
50g crystallised ginger, chopped (optional, or replace with fennel seeds)
2 eggs, lightly beaten, plus 1 egg for glazing
250ml milk
strawberry jam, to serve
400g clotted cream, to serve

Preheat oven to 220ºC/Gas Mark 7. Grease a large baking tray.

Sift the flour, baking powder, salt and ground cinnamon together in a bowl, then rub in the butter until the mixture resembles breadcrumbs. Stir in the sugar, sultanas, ginger and eggs. Stir in the milk with a wooden spoon, a little at a time, to form a smooth dough.

Roll out the dough on a lightly floured work surface to a thickness of 2cm. Dip a 5cm pastry cutter into a little flour and cut out the scones (be careful not to twist the cutter as this would cause the scones to rise unevenly). Re-roll the offcuts together and re-cut.

Beat the remaining egg in a bowl and carefully brush the tops of the scones, taking care not to let any run over the edge. Place the scones on the greased baking tray and bake in the preheated oven for 10–12 minutes, or until golden-brown.

Remove the scones from the oven and allow to cool slightly. Serve warm with strawberry jam and clotted cream.

CARDAMOM-SCENTED CUSTARD WITH DICED FRUIT

This home-style custard appears frequently on home menus and in hotel restaurants as well as street stalls pretty much all over the country. I remember this custard being served in St. Patrick's school in Asansol, too – it's one of the examples of Anglo-Indian cooking that we still see in circulation.

SERVES 4

900ml whole milk
½ vanilla pod, split lengthways
4 green cardamom pods, crushed
2 egg yolks
40g caster sugar

For the fruit
300g mixed chopped fruit, such as
    orange segments, diced apples,
    pears, bananas, green and black
    grapes
1 tablespoon caster sugar
juice of ½ lime
a few mint leaves, chopped (optional)

Mix together the chopped fruit in a bowl, season with the sugar, lime juice and mint and set aside to chill in the refrigerator.

Pour the milk into a non-stick saucepan (large enough to prevent it boiling over). Heat almost to boiling point, then turn down to a simmer and cook for 25–30 minutes until there is 300ml liquid left. Add the vanilla pod and crushed cardamom to the milk and allow to just come to the boil, then take the pan off the heat and leave to infuse for 30 minutes. Beat the egg yolks with the sugar in a large bowl.

Remove the whole spices from the pan of milk and discard. Reheat the milk until hot, then pour the hot milk over the egg yolks, whisking vigorously. When completely mixed in, place the bowl over a pan of simmering water and stir over a low heat for 10–12 minutes until the mixture thickens sufficiently to coat the back of a spoon.

Pour into a serving bowl, allow to cool and serve chilled with the fruit.

ENDING ON A SWEET NOTE

APPLE AND CAROM SEED CRUMBLE

This is a dessert we often make when our neighbours have a glut of apples in their garden. As you can probably tell by now, ajowan or carom seeds are a particularly favourite spice of mine, so here I go again! Carom seeds bring a wonderful pungency and savouriness to the dessert and give it added depth. They also aid digestion, so will come in handy burning off the sugar and butter, too.

SERVES 4

For the crumble topping
120g plain flour
60g caster sugar
1 teaspoon carom seeds
60g unsalted butter at room
   temperature, cut into pieces

For the fruit compote
300g cooking apples
30g unsalted butter
30g demerara sugar
¼ teaspoon ground cinnamon
100g blackberries

vanilla ice cream or custard, to serve

Preheat oven to 190°C/Gas Mark 5.

To make the crumble, tip the flour and sugar into a large bowl. Add the carom seeds and butter, and then rub into the flour using your fingertips to make a light breadcrumb texture. Do not overwork it or the crumble will become heavy. Sprinkle the mixture evenly in a thin layer over a baking sheet and bake for 12–15 minutes or until lightly coloured.

Meanwhile, for the compote, peel, core and cut the apples into 2cm dice. Put the butter and sugar into a medium saucepan and melt together over a medium heat. Cook for 3 minutes until the mixture turns to a light caramel colour. Stir in the apples and cook for a further 3 minutes. Add the cinnamon, stir and cook for another 3 minutes.

Cover the pan with a lid, remove from the heat, then leave for 2–3 minutes to continue cooking in the warmth of the pan. Sprinkle in the blackberries. Spoon the warm fruit into an ovenproof gratin dish and top with the crumble mix, then reheat in the oven for 5–10 minutes at 190°C/ Gas Mark 5.

Serve with ice cream or homemade custard.

WARM CHOCOLATE MOUSSE

This is a flourless version of a chocolate mousse which I have served in my restaurants for years and it's a great recipe to make at home too. It's easy to prepare and keep in the fridge until you're ready to serve. Simply bake in the oven for 8 minutes and you're done.

SERVES 8

325g dark chocolate (55%), broken into small pieces
50g butter, softened
6 eggs, separated
a pinch of ground green cardamom (or ½ teaspoon crushed roasted cumin seeds)
50g sugar

Place the chocolate and butter in a heatproof bowl set over a pan of simmering water and melt over a low heat, whisking regularly.

Meanwhile, beat the egg yolks in a separate bowl. When the chocolate has melted completely, mix the yolks and the cardamom or cumin seeds into the melted chocolate and stir well. Remove the bowl from the heat and set aside.

Prepare a meringue by whisking the whites and the sugar rapidly in a bowl until they form soft peaks.

Pour the chocolate mix into the bowl of meringue and mix evenly. Spoon the mixture into individual ovenproof bowls or coffee cups, filling them three-quarters full. Place in the fridge to chill for about 30 minutes before baking.

Preheat oven to 175ºC/Gas Mark 3 ½.

Place the moulds on a baking tray and bake in the preheated oven for 8–10 minutes. The mousse rises to the brim of the mould when done. Leave for a minute after removing from the oven. The centre of the mousse should remain soft and runny while the sides will set. Serve with an ice cream of your choice.

ENDING ON A SWEET NOTE

BASICS

CHAAT MASALA

Originally devised to give an extra zing and tang to 'chaats' in north India, this wonderful finishing spice is something most tandoori chefs can't and won't do without. There are several mentions of chaat masala in the recipes, so here's a recipe to make your own. It's also easily available in most good Asian grocery stores and online.

MAKES APPROXIMATELY 7 TABLESPOONS

1 tablespoon cumin seeds
1 teaspoon black peppercorns
¼ teaspoon ajowan seeds
1 teaspoon white pepper
¼ teaspoon ground asafoetida
1 tablespoon rock salt
2 tablespoons dried mango powder
1 teaspoon ground ginger
½ teaspoon garam masala
¼ teaspoon tartaric acid (optional)
½ teaspoon dried mint leaves, crushed
1½ teaspoons dried fenugreek leaves, crushed between your fingertips
1 teaspoon salt
1 tablespoon icing sugar

Heat a small heavy-based saucepan and dry roast the cumin seeds lightly over a medium heat for 2–3 minutes until the flavours just begin to release. The cumin should not be allowed to change colour or become too roasted. Allow it to cool down, then add all the other ingredients. Grind in spice mill and pass through a sieve. Stored in an airtight jar, this will keep for months. Sprinkled on kebabs or on salads, it adds a tangy, zingy flavour.

CHANA MASALA

This is a spice mix usually used to season chickpea curry but it works just as well with other beans or even mixed vegetables.

MAKES APPROXIMATELY 3 TABLESPOONS

1 tablespoon coriander seeds
½ teaspoon dried mango powder
½ teaspoon dried pomegranate seeds (optional)
1 teaspoon dried fenugreek leaves
4 cloves
1 teaspoon cumin seeds
½ teaspoon red chilli powder
1 bay leaf
1 teaspoon dried mint leaves, crushed to powder
⅛ nutmeg, grated
2 green cardamom pods

Dry all the ingredients for 30 seconds in a hot frying pan, then remove from the heat. Allow to cool, then grind to a fine powder. Store in a cool, dry cupboard in an airtight container away from direct light for up to 1 month. Use as specified in the recipe.

CRISP FRIED ONIONS

These are often used in biryanis and in some marinades, adding richness and depth of flavour to kebabs.

MAKES ABOUT 110G

600g onions, sliced
600ml vegetable or corn oil, for deep-frying

Heat the oil in a deep, heavy-based pan or deep fat fryer until medium-hot. Add the onions and fry in the oil until golden brown, then remove and drain on kitchen paper. Store in an airtight container for up to a week.

CURRIED YOGHURT

This is particularly good with the asparagus and gunpowder dish (see page 47).

1 tablespoon vegetable oil
½ teaspoon mustard seeds
4 curry leaves
½ teaspoon ground turmeric
1 teaspoon sugar
½ teaspoon salt
250g Greek yoghurt
2.5cm piece of ginger, finely chopped
1 green chilli, finely chopped

Heat the oil in a heavy-based pan to smoking point, then add the mustard seeds and curry leaves. When they start to crackle, quickly stir in the turmeric, sugar and the salt. Add this tempering to the yoghurt, along with the ginger and chilli and mix well. Adjust the seasoning before serving.

DRIED SHRIMP PASTE

Dried shrimp (used in Bengali Kichri, see page 61) is available in most good Asian stores. Simply blitz in a food processor.

GARAM MASALA

There are many versions of this hot spice mix; this is a good basic one. It is generally added to dishes towards the end of cooking to impart flavour, not to add heat as its name might suggest (*garam* means hot and *masala* means mix). If possible, I always recommend making your own garam masala. Commercial blends use a larger proportion of cheaper spices and less of the more expensive aromatic ones, such as cardamom and cinnamon.

50g coriander seeds
50g cumin seeds
20 green cardamom pods
10 cinnamon sticks, about 2.5cm long
2 tablespoons cloves
10 blades of mace
10 black cardamom pods
½ nutmeg
1 tablespoon black peppercorns
4 bay leaves

Put all the ingredients on a baking tray and place in a low oven (about 110°C/Gas Mark ¼) for 3–5 minutes; this intensifies the flavours. You could even dry the spices in a microwave for 20 seconds or so. Allow to cool, then grind everything to a fine powder in a spice grinder. Sieve the mixture to remove any husks or large particles. Store in an airtight container and use within 2 weeks.

GHEE

This is clarified butter, or the pure butter fat, clear and golden in colour. In India, ghee is traditionally made from buffalo milk, which is higher in fat than cow's milk.

The process involves souring milk to make yoghurt and then churning this to yield butter. However, unsalted butter made from cow's milk can also be used for ghee.

Ghee is the purest form of butter fat. In the days when there was no refrigeration, milk was converted to ghee to lengthen its storage life. Clarifying butter stops it from going rancid and it is also able to withstand high temperatures and constant reheating.

YIELD WILL BE APPROXIMATELY 200G

250g unsalted butter

Place the butter in a pan to heat. As the butter melts, let the liquid come to the boil. Simmer the melted butter for 20–30 minutes. Skim off and discard the froth that appears on the surface. The butter will separate into cooked milk solids, which will settle at the bottom of the pan, and clear, golden ghee at the top. Carefully pour off the ghee into a bowl.

As the liquid ghee cools, it will solidify, but will be creamy, like soft margarine. Ghee can be stored for up to a year if stored properly, i.e. in a cool dry, cupboard, away from contact with moisture.

GINGER AND GARLIC PASTE

Almost all savoury recipes require ginger paste and garlic paste, but there are certain dishes where more garlic than ginger is required. In that case, the pastes could be made separately.

MAKES ABOUT 8 TABLESPOONS

100g ginger, peeled
75g garlic, peeled

Chop up the ginger and garlic. Blend it to a fine, thick paste with 175ml water. Keeps in the fridge for up to 1 week.

ROASTING (AND CRUSHING) SEEDS

Put the seeds in a moderately hot dry frying pan or on a baking tray under a preheated grill and roast for a minute or two, until they are just dried, but not coloured. Remove from the heat, let cool slightly, then pound together using a pestle and mortar, until the seeds are crushed, but still coarse enough to be identified separately. If you want to grind the seeds to a powder, the best way to do this is in a spice grinder.

SPROUTED MOONG BEANS

200g whole green moong

Pick over and wash the whole green moong beans in cold water. Soak them overnight in plenty of water (around 5 litres). Strain the soaked lentils. Wet a couple of clean, thick tea towels in cold water and spread out on trays or wire mesh (such as a cooling rack). Spread the drained moong lentils on the wet towels in single layer and cover it with the second wet duster.

Transfer to a dark and dry place. Sprinkle the tea towel with more cold water every 6 hours so that it remains just damp. When you see the beans start sprouting (probably after 3–4 days), transfer the sprouts to a dry container and use within two days. Alternatively, use a germinator, available in most kitchen appliance stores.

BASIC TECHNIQUES

Handling and storing spices
Most basic spices, like cumin, coriander, red chilli and turmeric, are easily available ready ground. More aromatic spices, such as cardamom, cinnamon, cloves, mace and star anise, should preferably be bought whole and ground just before use. If stored in ground form, spices should be stored in air-tight containers, away from moisture and direct sunlight, and used within a month. Whole spices should be kept in the same way and used within six months to a year.

Marinades
It's difficult to say which was the original reason for people to start marinating meat, but our guess is that initially it was used to preserve and tenderise and, as people discovered how it enhanced flavour, more and more spices were introduced, creating the broad range of marinades used today.

Some people mix all the spices together and mix in the meat or fish, but I usually prefer to use the two-marinade method. Initially just salt, ginger and garlic pastes, and sometimes lemon juice, are applied and left until the meat or fish has absorbed their flavours. The second marinade contains a more complex mix of spices, plus yoghurt and sometimes cheese. Because a little moisture has been drawn out during the first marinating period, the meat or fish takes to the second marinade much better. This method of double marinating also contributes to complex layers of spices being created in the final dish.

Searing
This technique is not commonly used in kitchens in India, but at The Cinnamon Club, in our endeavour to use the best of all worlds, we use it quite often.

Searing is the process of sealing in the juices by placing the meat or fish on a hot pan or grill. In fact, some dishes like scallops are completely cooked this way, whereas other dishes, like venison, require further cooking in an oven or under a grill, or several minutes resting in a warm ambient place.

We also use this technique very effectively to recreate the tandoor cooking effect at home when a tandoor (see below) or barbecue is not available.

Tandoor cooking
In India, mostly northern India, meats, fish and certain vegetables are marinated and cooked on skewers in clay ovens, which are traditionally coal fired. Skewers rest on the sides of the oven, thereby exposing the meats or vegetables to intense heat from the coal flames. The juices that drip on to the burning coals create a smoke that imparts a characteristic flavour to the meat, fish or vegetable being cooked in the tandoor.

Tempering
This refers to the process of adding whole or broken spices to hot oil to release their flavours into it. Sometimes spices are also dry roasted to release their flavours, and then added to dishes to flavour them, but this is not tempering. In a lot of north Indian dishes, whole spices are added to hot oil or ghee in the beginning and then followed up with onions, tomatoes, garlic, ginger and other ground spices or spice pastes to complete the final dish. The process of adding spices may be referred to as tempering. However, some dishes like lentils or beans are finished by adding hot ghee or oil, which has been tempered with spices like chillies, cumin and garlic just before serving. This is often referred to as *baghar*.

GLOSSARY

ASAFOETIDA

Asafoetida is the dried sap from several species of giant fennel. Fresh asafoetida is a whitish colour and gradually turns pink to reddish brown upon exposure to air. It has an unpleasant smell (like pickled eggs) due to presence of sulphur compounds. On its own it tastes horrible, but when it is added to savoury dishes it completes the flavour of a dish. It is sold ground or as granules and can keep well for up to a year. It is supposed to be a cure for flatulence and is also prescribed for respiratory problems like whooping cough and asthma.

PEPPERCORNS

The berries of the pepper plant. India is the foremost producer of peppercorns, which are known as the king of all spice. Pepper can be used in all forms, from berry to dried form. It is sharp to taste and will spice up the dish. There are many varieties, with black and white peppercorns being the most widely found. The black peppercorn is the dried berry which is soaked, while the white version has simply had its skin removed. Pepper is used whole, crushed and ground. Freshly ground pepper is more flavourful. An infusion of peppercorns is good for sore throats, coughs and respiratory problems.

CARDAMOM PODS (GREEN AND BLACK)

This fragrant spice is very versatile and is used both in sweet and savoury dishes. There are many varieties of cardamom, the true one being green cardamom. Major producers are Sri Lanka, India, Guatemala and Thailand. It is the dried fruit of a herbaceous member of the ginger family. The fruits are picked just before they ripen and dried either in drying houses or out in the sun. The pods are shaped like oval capsules, containing hard dark brown seeds that are sticky and cling together. The best pod

varieties are a bright lime green colour, unblemished and unopened. It's advisable to buy fresh whole pods with freshness sealed in. It's usually a waste to buy ready ground cardamom, and much better to grind the seeds in a pestle and mortar just before using. Cardamom keeps well for up to 6 months if stored whole in dry, clean jars in a dark place. It also has medicinal properties and is used to relieve stomach disorders and heartburn.

CAROM SEED

Carom seed (also known as Bishop's Weed, and sold as Ajowan or Ajwain in Asian stores) is a close relative of dill, caraway and cumin. These tiny oval and ridged greyish-green seeds are curved and look a bit like miniature cumin. Usually sold in most Asian stores as whole seeds, it is used quite sparingly in cooking, so there's no need to buy too much. When chewed on its own, carom seed has a bitingly hot and bitter taste, and can leave the tongue feeling numb for a while. When cooked with other ingredients, its taste mellows. It is particularly good with fish and seafood dishes, root vegetables and green beans. Carom seeds are traditionally used as a cure for stomachache and over-eating.

CHILLI

Chillies are fruits of the capsicum species and have tranquil relatives like tomatoes and aubergine. They are cultivated mostly in tropical and sub-tropical countries. There are various different varieties available and the fieriness and pungency varies from one variety to another. When buying fresh chillies, look for crisp, unwrinkled ones that are waxy and green or red. Make sure they are bright and unbroken. For dried chillies, the fruits are picked when ripe and then dried in great mounds in the sun or in huge mechanical driers. As with most dried spices, powdered chilli loses its power and sparkle after a few months. Whole dried chillies can be stored for up to a year in a dark place. Exposure to light spoils the colour. Fresh chillies are a very high source of vitamins A and C.

CINNAMON

Cinnamon is actually an evergreen tree and part of the Laurel family. The dried inner bark of the tree is the spice used in cooking. The sweet, woody scent of cinnamon is very distinctive and the main flavouring for many desserts. Its taste is warm and sharply sweet and aromatic. Cinnamon is also used to flavour rice, curries and meats and is an essential part of the standard blend of garam masala (see page 225), the magic spice mixture of many popular rich and heady Indian dishes.

CORIANDER

Coriander is a herb with whitish pink lacy flowers, which mature into seeds. The tender leaves and pale green stems are used fresh. The seeds, which constitute the spice, are round and have fine ridges. The herb and spice are completely different from one another with regard to aroma and flavour. The leaves taste and smell fresh; the seeds, on the other hand, have a sweet, heady aroma with a subtle whiff of pine and pepper. Suitable for almost every savoury Indian dish, the spice and the herb are used daily in curries, chutneys, soups and drinks. Roasted ground coriander is an indispensable item in the spice box. Coriander infusion helps lower blood cholesterol and helps reduce fever.

CUMIN SEEDS

Cumin seeds look similar to caraway, but are puffed and light brown in appearance and the flavours differ. Cumin is cultivated in western Asia and the main producing countries are India, Iran, Indonesia, China and the south Mediterranean. The strongly aromatic aroma is characteristic and is modified by frying and roasting. Cumin is used whole or ground in many vegetable preparations and in tempering, and forms a major part in spice mixtures. Black or royal cumin seeds are dark brown, long and very thin and are found in central Asia and northern India. The seed's aroma is earthy and heavy, tasting nuttier when cooked. It is extensively used in Kashmiri and Mughal cuisine as a tempering for meats.

CURRY LEAVES

Curry leaves are available fresh or dried in most Asian stores. They come from a shrub which grows to about a metre in height or a beautiful tree which grows up to about 6 metres tall. Curry leaves are native to India and Sri Lanka and thrive in tropical climates. The almond-shaped green leaves have a strong curry-like odour; the taste is slightly bitter, but pleasant and aromatic. Curry leaves are an important ingredient in south Indian cooking and are used to flavour meats, fish, vegetables, breads and legumes. They are ground with coconut and spices to make chutneys. They have limited use in north Indian cooking where they are used mainly to flavour or temper lentils. Curry leaves were used in ancient Hindu ayurvedic medicines, the leaves and stem are used as a tonic, stimulant and carminative, and they can also be made into pastes to cure skin eruptions and bites.

FENNEL SEEDS

Fennel is the dried ripe fruit of a biennial or perennial herb known as *saunf*. They are small, green, cylindrical, are long, straight or slightly curved and have fine ridges. When dried they turn to a dull greenish yellow. Fennel is native to the Mediterranean, but also grows in other parts of the world. It is a common and much-loved spice in India. It adds richness to meat gravies, sweetness to desserts and special zest to vegetables. It is used powdered or whole; when dry roasted it grinds more easily. Fennel is also used in pickles and chutneys in north India. Fennel is available in any supermarket, either dried or fresh on stalks. Fennel has good digestive properties, which is why it is served after a rich Indian meal. It is one of the safest medicines for colic in babies.

FENUGREEK (DRIED AND SEEDS)

Known as methi, fenugreek is an annual that grows 50cm or so tall and is very easy to cultivate in mild climates. Fenugreek is grown around the Mediterranean, Argentina, France and India. Even in the west, a hot summer is enough to harvest a good crop.

The spice consists of small, hard, yellow rhombic shaped seeds. The whole plant has a pronounced, aromatic odour, with the seeds smelling of curry. It is quite bitter and is generally roasted to reduce this.

The seeds are available whole, crushed or powdered; the fresh stalk with leaves are sold in every Indian food shop. Dried fenugreek leaves, known as kasoori methi, are sold in packs and the best quality is from a place called Kasoor in Pakistan.

Dried fenugreek leaves are used to flavour all sorts of Indian savouries and curries. The fresh leaves are eaten in many ways and the dried seeds are widely used in southern Indian cookery in breads, chutneys, batters and lentils.

Ancient herbalists believed that fenugreek aided digestion. Even today the seeds are eaten to relieve flatulence, diarrhoea, chronic coughs and diabetes.

GARAM MASALA

Garam masala is a mixture of several spices roasted and ground to fine powder (see page 225). Many expensive spices go into the making of garam masala. Each region of India has its own version of garam masala depending upon the availability of spices, and the recipes change depending on individual taste, the proportions and the household. Garam masala has a rich, warm fragrance and tastes hot and aromatic. Commercially produced garam masala is not very aromatic and does not seem to retain its flavour for very long.

KASUNDI MUSTARD

Ready-made mustard commonly used in Bengali cooking. Mustard seeds are soaked in vinegar and made into a paste with mustard oil and dried raw mango. This prepared mustard brings its characteristic flavours to numerous dishes from the region.

LENTIL VARIETIES

Also known as dal.
Channa: sweet nutty flavour, these yellow lentils are the most popular lentils in India.
Masoor: salmon-coloured when dry, they cook quickly, and turn to a yellow purée.
Moong: mung beans, you can find them whole with green skins, or skinned and split. Yellow in colour and they cook quickly.
Toor: yellow in colour, and sometimes sold with an oily coating. Rinse this off before use.
Urad: comes in both black and white. The black has a strong, earthy flavour from the skins; used in robust dishes like Dal Makhani. The white skinless dal is mild and often used in conjunction with spices.

MUSTARD OIL

As the name suggests, mustard oil is extracted from mustard seeds. This oil is greatly flavoured favoured in Bengal and eastern India and certain Punjabi dishes get their flavour from this strong smelling, viscous, gold-coloured oil. It is normally heated almost to smoking point and cooled down before use in order to tone down its smell. People swear by its ability to promote thick, lustrous hair growth and it is often massaged into the scalp.

MUSTARD SEEDS

There are three main varieties of mustard – white, brown and black – and all three varieties grow in India. The seeds of the plant are the spice. White mustard seeds are pale tan in colour and have a smooth matte finish and are less hot when compared with the brown variety Black mustard seeds are larger than the other two, with seeds that are sharp, nutty, slightly bitter and aromatic in taste. Their heat is often misjudged, so be careful while adding them to recipes. Brown mustard seeds are also frequently seen in stores. The seeds are slightly smaller, the skin thinner and the flavour and heat in between the white and black seeds. Both brown and black mustard seeds can and are used interchangeably. Mustard paste has a strong flavour that hits you in the nose and then sings in your veins. In southern India and along the coast, mustard seeds are used for tempering. In Bengal mustard seeds are crushed to pastes and are used in fiery marinades and curries. Mustard is widely used for pickling.

NIGELLA

Seeds native to west Asia and the Middle East are now primarily grown in India. It is used in cuisine of all the regions, sprinkled on top of breads and has a light aromatic, peppery flavour. Toasting improves the flavour. Also known as kalonji or black onion seeds.

NUTMEG AND MACE

Native of Moluccas and imported by the Arabs, both nutmeg and mace are used in India. Nutmeg is enclosed in a shell, which in turn is surrounded by a lacy covering which is mace. Nutmeg is always used grated, it has a sharp flavour, generally used in rich dishes and also is a good digestive. Mace has a combined flavour of cinnamon and pepper and is similar to nutmeg, although much more subtle. Nutmeg and its oil is a good sedative if used with hot milk.

STAR ANISE

Star anise is the fruit of a tree in the magnolia family and grows mainly in China and Vietnam. Dried star anise is hard and has eight hollow boat-shaped petals, which form a perfect star and holds shiny seeds. Although it is not related to aniseed, the spice is similar in flavour, but the sweet aromatic taste is more prominent. It is generally used in rice dishes, teas and succulent meat curries. In some regions star anise is chewed to freshen breath and to help digestion.

STONE FLOWER MOSS

Stone flower moss or rock moss is a form of lichen, a dried moss that grows on stone. It is used in the same way as seaweed/ kelp in Japanese cuisine as a flavour enhancer. A little like a natural form of MSG (*ajinomoto*) in Chinese food, it does not have a taste of its own but is a great flavour fixer and when used in Indian food with several spices, it brings together the different spices and their flavours, with the end flavour being greater than the sum of its parts.

TAMARIND

Tamarind tree is a huge evergreen tree, which has small leaves and bears tamarind pods, which are string bean-shaped and brown with a thin, brittle shell. They grow up to 10cm long and contain a fleshy pulp held together by a fibrous husk. Within this are the brown seeds. Tamarind is soaked in warm water and the pulp is extracted. Nowadays tamarind pulp is readily available in many Asian stores. Tamarind is one of the main souring agents in Indian cookery. Tamarind is abundantly used in south Indian cookery in lentils, chutneys and curries. It is considered a mild laxative and is used to treat bronchial disorders. The name is a distortion from Arabic, Tamarind-e-Hind or Date-of-the-Indes.

TURMERIC

One of the most versatile and traditional spices used in Indian cooking, turmeric is the very heart and soul of any Indian curry with its earthy flavour. Turmeric is a member of the ginger family and grows best in tropical climates. India is the largest producer and exporter. Fresh turmeric root resembles ginger, which can be easily peeled. The roots are sold fresh, dried and powdered. It is ground turmeric that is generally used in cooking. Turmeric is used in virtually every Indian meat, lentil and vegetable dish. It is an excellent preservative, hence it is used extensively in pickles. It can be added to foods for its colour and taste or as a thickening agent. Turmeric is added sparingly to the cooking oil before the meat or vegetables are added and if it is not properly cooked, it leaves a pungent flavour. Turmeric is a very good antiseptic; consumption of it is said to help purify the blood.

YOGHURT

Yoghurt is a tangy, nutritionally excellent dairy product that can be made at home. The milk used contains a higher concentration of solids than normal milk. By increasing the solid content of the milk, a firm, rather than soft, end product results. Addition of non-fat dry milk (NFDM) is the method for doing this at home. Yoghurt is made by adding certain bacteria (starter culture) to milk, usually *Streptococcus thermophilus* and *Lactobacillus bulgaricus*. After inoculation, the milk is incubated at approximately 110°F until firm; the milk is coagulated by bacteria, producing lactic acid.

There are numerous varieties of yoghurt available on the market and one of them, Greek yoghurt, is usually thicker and more solid than the others, making it useful for marinades. Alternatively, natural yoghurt can be hung for 3–6 hours in a muslin cloth to drain off most of the water, thickening the yoghurt. Plain yoghurt, on the other hand, is used in sauces and dips where the thickness is not relevant – indeed the thinner the yoghurt, the longer it can be cooked without the fat separating.

INDEX

THANK YOU

Jon Croft and Meg Avent from Absolute Press. *Spice At Home* is their idea.

Matt Inwood and Lara Holmes – you make working on books enjoyable and a pleasure. Dare I say, I think I will struggle getting as much done in any other set-up. Matt and I make things difficult and Lara makes them look easy and beautiful. We make a good team.

Jo Harris, who provided many beautiful surfaces and receptacles to help make the food and photography look so wonderful.

Alice Gibbs, who has quietly and efficiently supported the entire process; most appreciated, Alice. Kim Musgrove, for her valued contribution to the design and artworking.

Genevieve Taylor painstakingly cooked each and every recipe at home to see if they worked and provided welcome feedback.

Gillian Haslam, for editing the whole work. She told me as she saw it and the book is much the better for it. Allan Jenkins and Howard Sooley, for the picture in the *Observer Food Monthly* a few years ago that kicked off the idea for Jon Croft.

Hari Nagaraj, Rakesh Nair and their team who have, aside from the help with prep and advice, provided me with the mind space to write this book.

To Sankar Chandrasekaran and Manoj Sharma, who stepped up to the plate to assist with the food photography and preparation. Boys, you did very well.

Abdul Yaseen, for giving up his office space for weeks at a time to let me write the recipes.

Shanna Manross, for sorting everything out all the time. You kept things together and me out of trouble. Thank you. Matt Inwood once told me, 'Shanna is probably the best Restaurant Assistant there is.' I have to say I concur.

To James Martin, Eric Chavot and all the other chefs who have invaded our household and changed our home cooking forever.

To my sister-in-law, Anisha, and my mother-in-law, Geeta, who you will see have contributed in shaping our home cooking in more ways than one. To Eshaan, Natasha and Maya – you are in part the reason why our cooking at home is so eclectic and interesting. You keep us on our toes.

My mum, who I can finally acknowledge after 24 years of professional cooking! A lot of my best ideas are actually yours.

Finally, to my wife Archana who makes our house a home. Your cooking is actually a lot better than most give you credit for. Without you, there wouldn't be a home, let alone *Spice At Home*.

THANK YOU.